Human

Behavior

A Beginner's Guide to Learn How to
Influence People

*(Understand Human Behavior Between
Rationality and Human Nature)*

Rachel Taylor

Published By **Darby Connor**

Rachel Taylor

*Human Behavior: A Beginner's Guide to Learn
How to Influence People (Understand Human
Behavior Between Rationality and Human Nature)*

ISBN   978-1-77485-623-9

Legal & Disclaimer

The information contained in this ebook is not designed to replace or take the place of any form of medicine or professional medical advice. The information in this ebook has been provided for educational & entertainment purposes only.

The information contained in this book has been compiled from sources deemed reliable, and it is accurate to the best of the Author's knowledge; however, the Author cannot guarantee its accuracy and validity and cannot be held liable for any errors or omissions. Changes are periodically made to this book. You must consult your doctor or get professional medical advice before using any of the suggested remedies, techniques, or information in this book.

Upon using the information contained in this book, you agree to hold harmless the Author from and against any damages, costs, and expenses, including any legal fees potentially resulting from the application of any of the information provided by this guide. This disclaimer applies to any damages or injury caused by the use and application, whether directly or

Table of Contents

Introduction

What are you seeing when you look into the mirror? What do you see in the mirror, regardless of your physical appearance? The short answer would be "I See Me." This answer is so complex and filled with interpretations, nuances, and adaptations that it is hard to give a concise answer.

When you look into the mirror or consider yourself, you are imagining what your impression of yourself is. Your perceptions of yourself are a reflection of what you have learned over time. This perception of yourself is a result of past experiences, biases or beliefs. The truth is only as accurate that wc believe. You will probably get a more accurate answer to the question, "Who am I?", if you include as many of your own responses as possible. However it is still important to keep in mind that perceptions are relative.

It is said that self identity can be fluid and flexible, but it is also highly malleable. How much can self identity be changed when confronted by contradicting opinions and evidence, how much? Is the core of our self-identity so hardwired that even though we have all the evidence and contradictory opinions, it is still impossible to alter?

Over the course of my entire life, I have been intrigued by the question "Who are we?" and "How did we get here?" Being self aware was an important aspect of my childhood. I strongly believe that being self aware is the key to becoming a happy adult. Making yourself aware of your inner world can be painful at times. It's easy to believe that our choices in personality, background and behavior are completely up to us. The truth is that it is far more complicated and difficult to believe than that.

In my quest of understanding myself as a human being and how it got there, I have explored many different areas in psychology. This book is the summation of my research thus far, and it also contains a guide for some of the most helpful resources that I have encountered on my journey.

I believe that in my efforts to fully define my self identity, I have found who I am and, to a degree, how I came up with this person. I hope this book will help you to embark on a similar journey. This is not a self-help guide. I don't claim that I know the answer to all your problems. However, I do believe what I have learned from my research will be of value to you: a deeper understanding human nature. Both you and me are human beings. In turn, I wish to help you get a better understanding.

This book does not focus on trauma and how it can be overcome. That would need to be the focus of multiple books. Instead, I'll be discussing how trauma could affect our personality and behaviour and the various types of psychotherapy. The best part about this aspect to me is whether these types of psychotherapy, though beneficial in treating trauma-related effects, are capable of altering our personality or behavior over the long-term.

There are many different ways to define personality type and I will go into each one in this book. This will let us ask: How much are personality types a part of who we really are?

Based on our self-awareness and past behavior, we might be able to pinpoint why we behaved the way we did in certain situations. Unfortunately, we often have difficulty identifying the root causes of our behavior, especially in cases where we regret it. I will discuss the connection between human behavior with the concept self-identity in the chapters that will follow. It is possible that by the final chapter, you will be able to understand both your own behavior and that of others far more effectively than ever before.

Chapter 1: Who Are You, Anyway?

"The question "Whom am I?" doesn't really have to get an answer. The question "Whom am I?" is meant for the questioner to disintegrate."

-- Ramana Maharshi

You can ask yourself what it is that you are trying determine when you ask who you really are. Most people answer this question with a sense if identity. Our identity is essentially a collection or experiences, memories, relationships with others, thought, and values that when combined create an understanding of who we as individuals. This human attribute, the necessity of identity when defining oneself, is fundamental. You can quantify your identity up to a point. You can break it down into pieces like:

Experiences

Valuations

Relationships

When we are able quantify something as humans, it makes us feel secure that it is clearly defined. Being able to quantify identity is an important step in answering the original question.

Every human being has a basic need for identification. Maslow's hierarchy includes this need, but it is likely that it falls under the second level. This is safety and security. These basic need do not necessarily have to be related to safety and security. Knowing that you are identified gives us psychological safety and helps us feel connected to others.

Science of Choice author Dr Shahram Heshmat believes "identity refers to our basic values which dictate the choices made (e.g. relationships, career). These choices reflect our core values and who we are." (Dennis. 2020).

This is not always the situation. Sometimes we make "outlandish" decisions. A straight A student may crash his father's car after a night of drinking. Is this a sign of his identity or not? At the other extreme, if a vicious killer stops a murderous rampage for the sake of saving a kitten from the drain, what does that say about his fundamental values?

Our identity is not only a combination of our values, beliefs, choices and decisions that we make internally, but it can also be affected by many external factors. Some of these factors we cannot control. Most importantly, our identities are not created by us. We are most likely to internalize the values taught to us by our parents or from the culture we grew up in. These values, and thus, our identity, don't always align with who we are. This is where the problem often arises.

It is possible to divide identity into organic or inorganic identities.

Our organic identity might be best described as our natural or personal character. It is the part our identity that stays the same regardless of where we were born or what we've done.

Our inorganic identification is the one that is created and essentially forced upon us by our circumstances, parents, and past experiences.

To further deconstruct the concept identity, although we share a common identity, it's fair to say we each portray different aspects depending on our roles. It is not surprising that our behavior and character at work will be different from when we interact with our spouses and families. Even if there are parts of who we are, they may not be visible to anyone.

This adaptation of identity to roles is normal. However, if it becomes a habitual process and we are convinced that the identity we show in one role represents an overriding truth about our self, then problems can arise. As we try and identify the truest version of ourselves, there may be an identity battle. The downside of this identity battle can be quite disastrous. It is no surprise that happy, content people also have a clear idea about their authentic self. They are also living lives that reflect that authentic self.

There is no doubt that finding your authentic self is a very personal process. Unfortunately, some people may never find the right answer no matter how much time they live. However, others will be able identify their authentic selves in a very young age.

So how do you find your true identity and live a life that reflects it? Psychologists recommend that this five-step process be followed.

1. Reflect: You don't have to make decisions here. This step simply requires you to sit down and be honest with yourself. How do other people see you? What are your opinions about yourself? Think about the comments people have made to you that really upset you. It is an indicator that someone is trying to point out something about you that you don't like. What do YOU like about yourself. What do you not like about yourself

2. Decide who you would like to become. There will always still be some distance between where you are now and what you wish to become. This step is about listing the traits that need to be improved.

3. Make active choices. The inorganic aspect of our identity has evolved mainly because we let ourselves be passive participants in the lives of others. We choose to maintain the status-quo out of fear, or because we think that it is the right choice for the role we are supposed to play. It is possible to find your authentic identity by making active choices to close that gap between who and what you are currently doing.

4. Exploring your passions is a great way to live authentically. These passions often get lost in the shuffle because they are too difficult to discover or because of the daily demands of life. These passions form part of who you are.

5. Take control of who you surround yourselves with. We are often dragged down

when we surround ourselves with people that don't match our authentic selves. If you find yourself often feeling isolated in a large group of people, then it is likely that those people are not the ones you should be surrounding you with. To strengthen our authentic selves, we need to surround ourselves only with people who reflect our true identity and value.

Do Identity Variations Affect Each Other?

Absolutely! It is a continuous process that creates our human identity. This process continues as we move through life and encounter new experiences. One woman who may have characterized herself as timid and meek when she was in her 20s may discover that by her 40s she has no desire to use those words. It could be her discovery of her true identity, it could also be the evolution of her identity.

This is a sign that identity changes over time. This suggests that instead of asking us who we are, we should consider how we would like our lives to be in the moment.

The Breaking Down Process

We will have to be able recognize the differences between our true selves and the traits we have adopted to fit our needs.

This is a difficult process that can take time and is not easy to do. However, it is crucial to be able to give up these false aspects of ourselves in order to live a true life.

It is common for the unauthentic aspects of your personality to be most evident in the choices you make. If you're making happy decisions, then it is likely that you are using authentic elements of your identity. If you are making choices that make you feel unhappy, these are likely to be influenced by parts of your authentic identity.

Aspects Of Identity

Identity can be expressed in many different ways by different schools.

Psychologists define identity as being related to our self-image, individuality, or self-esteem. Peter Weinreich, a psychiatrist, defines identity to include "the totality one's self conception," that is, how one interprets themselves as they were in the past. Also included in this definition is ethnic identity. This describes how we construe our ancestral past and our aspirations for our future ethnicity.

Gender identity affects how we perceive ourselves. It is also an aspect of our human identity. Our gender identity has a direct impact on how we see ourselves and our relationships with other people, ideas, nature, and others. Gender identity has one of the greatest impacts on our lives. This is because it influences how we see ourselves in relation to other people, ideas, and nature. Recently, there has been an increased acceptance of many different gender identities. People feel more comfortable to explore this aspect.

Other aspects of identity include:

Racial Identity: This is the part of identity that is not often chosen. Although racial distinctions are primarily political constructs, humans have developed over time to identify with particular racial groups according to their skin color. Racial identity can be beneficial in that it provides a sense or belonging. But it can also be detrimental to those who feel they don't belong within a particular racial groups.

Religious identity: This aspect is possibly the most fluid. While we will probably be born with one religious identity, this identity will only last for the first years of our lives. Later, as our personalities mature, we may choose to adopt a new religious identity. Certain groups have a greater importance in religious identity than others. People who are forced to follow a certain religion can experience identity conflict.

Ethnicity: Although closely tied to racial Identity, this aspect can be more fluid over time than racial Identity. Ethnicity simply refers the degree to which we adhere to the cultural values, traditions, and attitudes that are part of our ethnicity. Although we cannot choose the specific ethnicity or number of ethnicities in which we are born, our adulthood makes it more possible to adhere to this aspect. Children born to multiple ethnicities can often identify with the dominant one, which will become part of their identity. As they get older they may feel a stronger attachment to another ethnicity and could struggle to identify with that heritage.

Occupational identity. While this aspect is less important than the greater part of our identity for most, it can be a major component of some people's human identity. This is common in occupations requiring great commitment and danger such as within the army or police. It is possible for people to identify with an occupation even after they have stopped participating in it.

The role of social psychology and identity will be discussed in more detail in this book. At this point it is pertinent that sociology places a great deal of importance on the roles we play in society. An identity negotiation may occur whereby a person talks to society about what role they need to play in defining their identity.

While psychologists use the term "identity", to refer to the distinctive characteristics of a person, sociologists tend to focus on how our views of ourselves can be affected by a variety of memberships within the society. Social psychologists know that even if two people have identical memberships, they will not be able to give the same description of their identity. This is because each individual reacts to the various roles they play in society in their own way. Therefore, each person will judge the importance and relevance of each role in their personal identity differently.

Neuroscientists apply all of the above to identify human identity and attempt to understand how it is represented in biological form within the brain.

Weinrich's Identity Structure Analysis

Peter Weinrich, British psychologist and pioneer in human identity analysis, was an innovator. His life's work included the development and implementation of the Identity Structure Analysis. The ISA is described to be a powerful and unique method of understanding and analyzing human identity development and formation. Weinrich invented the system, and developed Ipseus software to assist in analysis. The ISA draws from a range disciplines, including sociology, psychology and social anthropology. It examines how psychological and societal influences shape the individual human identity, as well as how it is affected and influenced by the social environment in which they live.

The ISA Framework is based on the fundamental assumption that human beings have a social, agentic, or developing nature. It also assumes that we continuously reframe and rethink our identities based in response to changes in society and personal experiences. Ipseus allows us to empirically delineate the mixture of all of these elements and changes. Weinrich was sadly lost in 2016, but his work is still being done by psychology students. These students continue to use Ipseus, ISA and other tools to get empirical data about human identity (Stapleton - 2016).

Online Identity

An aspect of identity that psychology's founder fathers may not have considered, but is still relatively new, is the online identification. This is the topic of current research, and the results so far are quite fascinating. If you've ever used social media for any length of your life, you might have been amazed by the insights you made about people you actually know. Mary, your cousin, for example, is an extremely quiet person but can comment with the most arrogant voice about the topics she loves. These same topics are often discussed at family gatherings. However, Mary isn't nearly as passionate in her defense of her position online. Mary could have many personalities. She is only being impacted online, just like millions of people.

This effect results in uninhibited, unwise, often uncharacteristicistic behavior on the internet. It is caused by audience gratification, an assumption of anonymity, and an uninhibited, unwise character. This behavior could be compared to the way an individual would behave when under the influence. The behavior is often regrettable the next morning.

An online identity is entirely self-crafted. It may be the one place where an individual can show their ideal identity without restriction, especially if they don't include any personal identifying information.

This distinction in identities online and offline can be dangerous, but it can also be beneficial in many cases. Online identity can sometimes "leak" into offline identities, which allows individuals to more fully live out their authentic identity. This often happens when individuals are unable to live their authentic identity in offline life due to societal pressures. When people get support online while being authentically their gender or sexual identities, it can often be enough to help them find their courage and accept those identities in their actual lives.

It is more often that the individual shares their "secret personality" with the world than that it is about realizing that they are part a large, global group of people who identify in the exact same way. It can be quite isolating feeling like some aspects of your identity should be hidden because of fear of rejection, reprisals, or violence. To reduce isolation, you need to find a community that supports your authentic self.

More Thoughts about Define Identity

To develop a definition for identity, we might start by looking at the core issue of the term "identity", regardless of how it might be conceptualized. The core issue of identity, whether it is implicit or explicit, involves people's responses to the question: "Who are you?" This sounds basic, but hides a lot.

First, it's important for you to know that identity can refer not only to the self-definitions but also to pairs, small groups and larger social groups.

The question can be asked to self introspectively or to the group. as well as within and between groups. Your identity, in other words, is not just what you think or believe you are, either as an individual/collective or as an entity, but also what you do in intergroup or interpersonal interactions. This includes the social acceptance or rejection received from these actions by other groups and individuals. In reality, however, the concept is made up of many related contents and process. These are explored in various areas of study and metatheoretical perspectives. However, the definition of identity is not limited to all features that can be used as a way to identify someone.

The term identity is often used in public and scholarly discourse to describe biological characteristics.

But, just because someone has a British passport does it not automatically make them British citizens.

These characteristics do not make up part of your identity.

It is therefore not a study on identity, even though it examines two areas that people often use to describe themselves. A study of identification, by contrast, is undoubtedly a study in identity. This study attempts to clear such disparities through individuals stereotyping their self in terms the dominant cultural representations of men or women.

Identities approaches currently in use focus on one or several of the following three "levels" at what identity can be defined:

personal (relational), collective (collective). Partly, the distinction between personal, collective, and relational identities can also be seen as a distinction among different forms of identity. But, it is also known that different mechanisms are used over time to form, sustain, or alter identities. Individual, relational and collective identities are often distinguished by a focus on identity creation and transformation. Although this is not necessary, it is common for theories to emphasize these processes.

A person's personal identity or individual is the way they define themselves. These could be goals, principles, and beliefs. Religious and moral beliefs. Behavioral and decision-making parameters. Self-esteem. Personal identity theories are not only focused on individual-level identity material but also emphasize the individual's agentic role when establishing or finding their identity.

Relational identity refers the one's identity when it is related to others, such as child or partner, parent, boss, boss, client, and co-worker. Relational identification is not limited to these positions. It also includes how people perceive and view them. Many ideas suggest that identity is established and situated within interpersonal space, within families or in the roles that one plays in a larger context of relational identities processes. One common thread is that these views believe that identities can't be formed by individuals. People who claim to have a particular identity must accept their claims.

Collective identity describes the association and behavior of individuals with social groups and other social categories. Collective identity can be defined as membership, which may include race, religion and gender in any type of social category or group.

Perhaps our idea of identity can seem much more wide-ranging now that it includes significant others, social role models, face-toface groups, and other broad social categories. However, it's important to expand the definition of identity. William James famously said that a person's material identity includes not only his mind, body, friends and spouse but also his clothing, home, vehicle and bank account contents. The idea is that people not only view and treat social bodies other than their own as part of themselves, but also as material objects. It is possible to call individuals material identities beyond human, relational or collective identities.

These dimensions of identification can form the basis for an integrated organizational notion of identity. The following dimensions of identity, as seen from the perspective of an individual, are the result of the person's self-chosen and ascribed commitments as well personal attributes and convictions. Roles and positions in relation of important others. Her membership in social group and category (including both her own group status and that of the wider context); Schwartz et al. (2012).

Identity's Derisive Properties

Sometimes our identities create problems, but they can also divide us, instead of promoting inclusion. How can we be divided by our identities? How do they divide us?

Labels serve two purposes. To distinguish us from other people and to be able to support people who feel like they are excluded. We seek self-definition through separation from others.

Let's not forget this thought: If we keep looking at ourselves through the lense of exclusion aren't our thoughts simplifying and judgmental? Is it ever possible for labels to be used to identify you, rather than as an identity, but as you are an individual?

The labels we use to define ourselves do not reveal the complexity of our individuality or what it means for us to be human. We use labels to glorify ourselves, hide from others, and victimize our own selves. Incontinence is often defined as quick and simplistic identification. A long list of labels is used by everyone to identify themselves. It's like marking boxes on a sheet. It will include information about your gender, race/ethnicity, sexual orientation and abilities as well any other relevant information. These labels are variations on a simpler vocabulary of classification: nerdy. It could be one of them against us. Even though they might identify as the same groups as yours, their intersectional experience will be different.

Demographic identities, while not being a definition of who we really are, are just aspects of who and what we are. These identities do not reflect our dreams or favorite books, senses, humor, best friends, or the many other things that make us unique. Your cultural heritage is part of your story. This is different from subscribing in a collective identity. Sometimes, it helps us avoid the painful task of trying to discover who we really are. By valuing others' affinity with a fictitious collective rather than their individuality, we can disrespect and reduce our relationships. It is important that you remember when considering identity that these labels don't define a person.

The commonality of a person being classified as another can often lead to the loss of our individuality. It also makes it difficult for people to get along with one another. People are fundamentally different. However, we sometimes forget that our fundamentally similarities are what makes us human. The only term that really refers to anything is "human being." We all share certain human experiences and are therefore endowed with the ability of understanding each other as human beings. It is the essence of human nature to have empathy and compassion, and share in our shared experiences and understanding. It transcends the social limitations that we all create and allows us to feel the need to care for strangers. The world may judge us according to our identities. So why shouldn't the rest accept it? However, it's more powerful to seek out what we have and not focus on what is different. Reducing ourselves to only our identities is bad for us in two ways. First, when we adhere to a collective we overlook individuality. Second, when we hold on to what divides we we forget what we share in common.

I do not mean to denounce identity. It is crucial, however, to use it for celebrating who we are.

An arbitrary label I am given by circumstance does not define identity. That is not an identity. Identity should reflect your inner self. And no one but you can determine that. We cannot change the majority of the labels we are given. It is possible to change the way that we interact with these labels. Understanding you as a reader is not dependent on the group or demographic that you identify most with. You are not limited to the identities you own. There is more to your identity.

This chapter will discuss a variety definitions and theories of identity that are being used by different schools. We now have a better idea of what identity means for humans and how it develops and changes over the years.

In the next chapters, we'll explore the relationship between personality and identity. We also will try to understand different personality types.

Chapter 2: Different Personality Types

As we understand the concept human identity, we need to also examine the personality overriding label we often give to our identity.

What is the relationship between personality and identity? Is your personality as fluid as you have an identity?

Personality Typing

If you have spent any amount of time studying personality types, then you are likely to have found that there are many personality types. Each test also has its own name.

While this might be confusing for the average person, it can help you see how many personality tests are similar. The major differences between these personality tests are their focus and the area they target.

Personality Typing Development

Hippocrates suggested in about 460 BC that humans have a persona'. This is a character which consists of four distinct temperaments. He said that people's humor and personality were determined by what fluid was dominant.

Withelm Witt became the "Father" of Psychology in 1879.

In the late 1800s, the psychodynamic approach was introduced. This revolution changed the way that we interpret personality among groups of people.

Sigmund, Freud, was the original founder of this approach. He believed that our personalities are more complex that what was initially proposed. That our actions and personalities are driven by our underlying desires and needs.

Carl Jung stated that the human personality is a combination of four distinct preferences: intuition, feeling (thought), sensation and feeling (feeling). The rise of personality testing and typing in the 1900s was especially noticeable in the workplace.

The Woolworth personal profile sheet, which was the first modern personality testing tool, was invented by the American Army of the United States. This was used to detect which recruits could be exposed to shell shock.

Since the 1900s, personality theories, personality assessment, and tests for humans have grown exponentially. Many personality quizzes are now common, such as those that test your personality, like the 16-personas test or the Myers-Briggs testing, the big 5 and other IQ test.

Top 6 Personality Tests

1. DiSC

Walter Clark introduced the DiSC personality assessment in 1940. This profile measures superiority, power steadiness, conscientiousness and superiority. The questionnaire was designed specifically for organizational use. It can also be used for managing employee growth, sales training or dispute management, team building as well customer services, communication, and job coach.

There are 28 questions for the DiSC review. For each question, the individual selects the most similar word to them. The DiSC review is simple to use and administer. It can also be delivered quickly.

DiSC uses 4 components of personality to identify types

Dominance is a trait that identifies people who are strong-willed, determined, results-oriented, direct, and powerful.

Influence: Such people are outgoing.

Conscientiousness. Such people are reserved and precise.

Steadiness is a trait that shows the ability to be patient, even-tempered, understanding, accommodating, humble, and tactful.

Each person is unique, and there are four aspects to the DiSC personality types.

2. 16 Personality Factor Questionnaire (16PF)

Tatsuoka, Cattle, and Eber published 16PF in 1949. But, since its initial publication, additional information has been added. The questionnaire was based on Allports4000 personality traits. Cattle shortened the results to 171, 16 and 16 respectively, to make the design of the method. It can be used to assess common behaviors and is useful for selecting team members, career guidance, therapy, marital counselling, and other clinical purposes.

It measures abstractness.

3. HEXACO Model Of Personality Structure

The HEXACO dimensional personality test was developed in 2000. It also tests theoretical interpretations of previous studies. The model assesses six key dimensions of personality: honesty, humility, extraversion and pleasantness.

4. Revised NEO People Inventory

Costa and McCrae designed the Updated NEO Personality Inventory. This was done in the 1970s and then completed in 2005. It is used to quantify and evaluate the Big-5 traits that are outlined in a five-factor model, which includes openness and knowledge, conscientiousness and extraversion.

For instance, neuroticism could be defined as: anxiety, aggression or depression, self consciousness, impulsiveness and susceptibility. The inventory also includes six subcategories that correspond to each of the five characteristics. Extraversion refers to the subcategories that include warmth, gregariousness. assertiveness. movement. Finding stimulation and positive emotion are also included.

5. Myers-Briggs Type Indicator

Isabel Briggs Myers created the Myers-Briggs Type Indicator with Katharine Burn Briggs (MBTI) during the 1940s.

The test is based a Carl Jung hypothesis. It posited that four psychological processes are used by humans to affect their perception of the world. These four psychological mechanisms are intuition and sensation as well as thought and feelings.

Myers-Briggs assesses how information is processed. The questionnaire results are used to determine which personality the participant is, with each having their own strengths and weaknesses.

6. Merril Wilson Personality Breakdown

Merril Wilson personality typing may be one of the most simple and straightforward ways to identify a person.

These four personality styles include Driver, Amiable (verbal), Amiable (logical), and Amiable (logical). There are two variables to help classify personalities: are they better at data and facts? Or are they better at relationships. They may also be introverted, extroverted, or both.

Driver-Extrovert Reality Dependent

Analytical Introvert based in reality

Partnership Amiable/Introvert

Expressive-Extrovert partnership

Major and minor forms would exist for most people. The key is to determine the major form of each type and to communicate that information to others.

Types of personalities based on the Merril–Wilson breakdown

There are four major personality categories if we use the Merril Wilson personality typing break down:

Driver

Drivers are powerful people. They have a strong will to succeed and a willingness to do whatever it takes. They can often appear dominant and move quickly. Their bad side is they can sometimes come across as stubborn and arrogant. You may find your personality aggressive, pushing for others and trying to get things done.

Analytical

It is very likely that you have an elevated level of Analytical typing, if you are reading this book. Analytical styles continually analyze, weigh out the pros and cons and make lists. Analytical styles can be so thorough that they almost have too many details. They are always asking questions. They are often praised by others for their creativity and talent. They may suffer from paralysis, overthinking or paralysis. If you've ever made a list that "does things the right" then you are an analytical.

Expressionist

These people are "natural" people. They love to socialize and chat. They are great storytellers and often over commit themselves to satisfying others. They are skilled at conveying vision and getting people excited by ideas and problems. They can sometimes be unreliable when it involves getting things done.

Amiable

Amiable types can be the quietest and most difficult to sedate. They seem calm and unaffected. They can wait until the last possible moment to make a decision or simply agree to follow the example of others. They are extremely emotional people and seek only peace. They will do whatever it takes to avoid conflict with others or upset them.

Personality Types Based On the Myers-Briggs Breakdown

The personality types according to Myers-Briggs are broken down into four distinct dichotomies.

The four dichotomies are a series of opposed features intended to show certain aspects or characteristics of a character. There are:

Introversion verses Extroversion

Sensing vs Intuition

Thinking vs Sentiment

Judging vs. Perception

Introversion verses Extroversion

This is a dichotomy about energy management. Resources claim they are correct. However, it's possible to simplify and offer misleading explanations as to how energy is managed.

This is an example.

This doesn't seem like it's associated with the introverted Introvert who likes being in large crowds, or the Extrovert that can't seem fast enough to leave a crowd.

Introversion and extroversion are actually different in how they view their "real", world. Introverts call the "real universe" their inner universe. Extroverts live in the "real universe", which is the world outside of themselves. This placement of reality is what leads to many different behaviors, whether we are extroverted or introverted.

Introverts may pause briefly before speaking. They will also talk as if they are thinking, which allows them to hear it from others and assess its validity. Extroverts, on the other hand, are more introverted. They are often able to talk while they think, because they can listen to their thoughts and assess their validity.

An introvert's inner world will not always match the external world. Introverts are in a position where they can continuously analyze data and link it with their internal beliefs. Sometimes, this can get tiring. Eventually, time is all that is needed to rest.

An introvert creates an exception by making room in their inner universe for another person. This occurs when they have a strong bond or find a friend. The Introvert enjoys being involved in the inner world of another person. They are not at odds, but rather part of that inner world.

Extroverts find it easier to feel at home when they engage with the world around them.

They find variety stimulating and are drawn to it as a rule. They become lonely and anxious if they are spending too much time by themselves. To be able to feel connected, they must spend some time with their environment. Connection with others does not necessarily mean that they must be. It might be enough to simply walk around, take out the camera, or find interesting items.

Extroverts can become lonely if they spend too much time together. They don't mean any disrespect to their loved ones but they can become restless, and want to go out into the world.

Introverts could become defensive and bashful of their energy after years of adapting to the outside world. Extroverts need to find new energy. They may recognize the value of other people's energy and knowledge. However, each person is unique and different individuals may exhibit extravert and/or introvert behaviors.

Sensing vs Intuition

Next, the Myers-Briggs four-letter-code dichotomy deals with how you see your universe. Sensors want data reliability; intuitives prefer pace and depth.

First, intuitives have learned to trust patterns. They can quickly recognize hidden connections between items and interpret it. They are comfortable thinking about and speculating about the future. They simply extrapolate meanings from a few data points.

Sensors have the same power but don't trust it. They don't try to hone this skill. Instead, they rely only on facts that are reliable and can be verified in real life. They are able to master both their own history and that of others. Sensors often learn quickly to control objects and respond quicker than others. This makes them appear to be in the present. They are able to see the truth right in front them and don't have to doubt it. Sensors understand that truth is reliable and speculation not.

Additionally, the relationships between sensors and intuitions over time are quite different. If the only thing that sensors care about is accurate, current, and solid data, then past and present contexts can be very relevant. Sensors can't be reliant on events that haven't occurred. The future is far more important. Intuitives on the other side are comfortable with what is not. They do not view the past as anything other than a reference point that will guide them in their future projections.

The Sensor/Intuitive dichotomy also alters principles and fundamental wants. Sensors believe that values such family, tradition, enjoying life, being present, sensitive, and staying on top of current affairs are embedded in the informed, knowable and can be trusted. Intuitives rely primarily on the abstract as values: meaning making, narratives creativity, possibilities and perspectives, and asking questions like "what if?"

Intuitive and sensors both play a major role in our world. Sensors are responsible for managing and maintaining the infrastructure that keeps us moving as a collective. Intuitives are generally considered to be the pioneers. Their innovative ways of looking at things lead to new paradigms. This makes sense as there is less need for intuitives. Without creativity, everything could go to pieces. The world would be stagnant if there was no creativity.

Thinking vs Feeling

The third dichotomy, which is a four-letter Myers-Briggs classification, deals with how decisions are made and knowledge is assessed. For assessing the value of a concept/citizen/object, Thinkers use impersonal metrics while Feelers use human-based and intimate considerations. All the Thinkers are sound, but all the Feelers think. The same way that Thinkers use their brains and logic to arrive at their conclusions, so too will Feelers. Thoughters also use emotion-based factors to evaluate their principles.

A Thinker's belief system can be used to assess their emotions. It can show how annoyed they get when others disregard what they believe is right. If their metrics aren't being met, it can be emotionally taxing for the Thinker. Feelers, by contrast, will often ignore their feelings in an effort to maintain the status-quo. They value social considerations and it is not uncommon to feel compelled to keep peace in difficult situations.

It makes sense for Thinkers to have more data and measurement on their minds. They will be more relaxed and professional in all aspects of careers, partnerships, or other situations that require the management and use of data and resource. To the same extent, Feelers will keep people and human interests in mind but would feel more comfortable displaying emotion and interpersonal dynamics.

Judging vs Perceiving

The fourth and final dichotomy within the four-letter Myers-Briggs system is about how you organize your universe. Perceivers are responsible for organizing their inner world to permit freedom in outer space, while Judges manage their outer world to ensure liberty within it.

Judges like to be free in their mind and wander through the garden. They think the same as fish in a pond. In order to concentrate or see their thoughts clearly, Judges need quiet. Interrupting an intellectual Judger is like causing the water to boil. All the ideas are lost and the Judge might not be capable of getting them back.

This helps the Judger maintain a balance of power over their environment. They must be vigilant against any future disturbances. The basic need to think becomes an all-encompassing need to have order in the world. Judges also state that they think better when their home is clean and clear of visual clutter. It is often easier to maintain a clean house than to organize their work desk and private rooms.

Perceivers can see the opposite. Their thoughts and emotions are well organized. Perceivers can be interrupted at any time during their thought process, but they usually save the information and tag it later. It's as simple as finding the right mental bookmark to store it. However, some Perceivers don't know this phenomenon. They are able to arrange thoughts and emotions, but they don't know it. Judges, on other hand, are more aware that there is no internal structure. This might be because they get annoyed by being distracted and lose track of their thoughts.

Perceivers' ability to organize and track thoughts allows them to participate in improvisation, their favorite pastime. Perceivers want to feel completely free to do what they like in the world. Perceivers should be able to take quick decisions if their goal is to improvise or maximize on possibilities.

Although Judgers have a tendency to be quick-witted they are not the best improv comedians. This suggests that they may not be too worried about disrupting their lives, so it is possible to put household organizations on the back burner. It is a common trait among Perceivers to throw clothes around in the wrong places, creating a "floordrobe."

Another common trait among Judgers is their ability to schedule. If a Judger does not have the ability to act spontaneously and improvise, it is likely that they will feel uncomfortable in situations they do not anticipate. A Judger who has a good idea of what's ahead will feel more relaxed. The happier a Judger will be, the more prepared they can be. Even though Perceivers can benefit from preparation in certain situations, they will be able to excel even when there is pressure. They are prone to procrastinating on projects and tasks. They have learned through experience that they excel in the eleventh hour. Judges will often use the same last-minute processes to produce their worst work and are usually inefficient.

Judges can become confused and have their thoughts locked up, while Perceivers can pull out a rabbit from a hat when they need it. They would not identify themselves this way.

There are instances when Judges can be careless or disorganized while Perceivers are organized and meticulous. A Judge might have a neat and orderly life but a chaotic room. This is because nobody can see them except themselves. The return on investment for cleaning their bedroom might not motivate them. A Perceiver might see clean houses or cars as more valuable than others, and they might not want to be without any object. These are exceptions and are more related to the cognitive functions of a person than to their personality type.

The Possible Combinations

According to the Myers-Briggs personality Typing, there are 16 combinations of the dichotomies mentioned in this chapter.

Dodge, 2018).

Personality Traits

Personality traits describe people's typical thoughts, emotions, and behaviors. Personality traits can be described as stability and consistency. Trait psychology assumes that people's individual traits are not the same. They differ in terms of their position on a set trait dimensions that have remained constant over time. The Five-Factor Model of traits is the most widely-used. This model includes five general traits that can all be identified with the acronym OCEAN (Openness, Conscientiousness. Extraversion. Agreeableness. And Neuroticism). Each of these major traits can easily be broken down into individual facets, which allows for a more detailed analysis about a person's personality. Some trait-theorists claim that there are additional traits that cannot be fully captured by the Five-Factor Model. Critics argue that people react differently to different situations and that the traits concept is not a good idea. A major topic in the field revolves around the relative power and influence of people's personality traits on their behavior. Although there are many theories about personality, Gordon Allport (and other "personologists") claimed that the best way to see the differences among people is by understanding their personality characteristics. Personality traits represent the fundamental dimensions that define how people differ. According to trait psychologists there are only a limited number these dimensions (dimensions like Extraversion or Conscientiousness). Each individual can fall anywhere on each dimension. That means they could be low on a particular trait or medium on it.

There are three factors that can be characterized as personality characteristics: (1) consistency (2) stability (3) individual differences

1. Individuals need to be consistent across situations when they use a personality trait. One example is that they may be talkative at home but not at work.

2. Individuals who possess a trait show some stability in their behaviors over time. At age 30, a person who is talkative will become more talkative after age 40.

3. Individuals have different behavior patterns. Talking is not an individual trait. Walking on two-feet is also not. Individuals differ on how active they are and how often they talk, which is why personality traits such as Talkativeness (or Activity Level) exist.

The Congruence Of Personality And Identity

Now that you have an understanding of identity and of the various personality types of humans we are able to see how they relate.

We all know that identity is something that we give to ourself. It's the sum of all our values, morals, as well our legal and physical circumstances. Personality refers to how we act out our identities. Our personality traits show aspects of who we are.

Some aspects of the personality of someone you know may be recognizable, such as funny, charming, intelligent or funny. Each person adapts and changes over time. But your identity changes less often. Individuals are made up of identity and personality.

Our individuality and uniqueness as humans is the result of a fusion of personality and identity. While you may have the same identity as another person, your personality will be completely different. This makes you unique.

Chapter 3: Emotion and human perception

Human perception and emotion are typically seen as two distinct fields of study. The truth is though that they are very closely related. The way we perceive the world often depends on the emotions we feel and vice versa. So far, we've discussed the concept identity and the different personality categories into which we can fall. A study of the psychology of human behavior cannot be complete without the additional "padding" around identity and personality--emotions and perceptions.

This chapter will focus on the psychology of emotions as well as human perception. It will explain how these two aspects of the human experience interact to create our behavior.

What is Human Perception (Haperception)?

Perception refers the ability to organize, recognize and understand sensory data so that you can reflect and comprehend what is happening in the world.

These impressions are based on impulses that move through your nervous system. This stimulation can be either physical or chemical. Vision is, by way of example, light hitting the retina. Smell, on the other hand, is mediated using molecules of odor. Hearing, however, involves waves of pressure.

Perception is not simply passively received signals. It also is influenced by the learning memory, anticipation and attention of its receiver. Sensory Feedback is a method that transforms low-level signals into higher-level ones. This is how concepts, perceptions or knowledge, restorative or selective mechanisms (such like attention) and perceptions of an individual can be linked to affect perception. Perception is dependent upon complex nervous system processes. However this processing is subconscious and often effortless.

Since the 19th century birth experiment psychology, Psychology's view of perception has changed through the use and combination of many approaches. Psychophysics quantitatively defines the relationships between sensory inputs and physical characteristics of perception. Sensory neuroscience studies how neural pathways underlie perception. It is possible to also study perceptual system in computational terms. Perceptual problems can be defined as the degree to that sensory stimuli such a smell, color or sound occur in empirical reality and not in the mind.

Although senses have traditionally been seen as passive receivers, brain research has shown that perceptive systems in the brain actively and pre-consciously attempt to make sense. It is still controversial whether perception is an actual process of hypothesis testing, and whether or not practical sensory information makes this unnecessary.

The brain's perceptual capabilities allow people to see the surrounding environment as constant, even though it is constantly changing and incomplete. Human brains and animals are organized modularly. Different sensory input types are processed by different parts of the brain. Some of these modularities take the shape of sensory maps. They link a section of the brain with a specific aspect of its environment. All these modules are interconnected and can impact one another. One example is taste.

What is emotion?

Emotion can be defined as a complex experience of emotion, including behavioral experiences and perceptions. This is what gives meaning to a particular state of affairs or event.

Aristotle, a Greek philosopher wrote that emotions are all feelings that can so change people as to alter their judgments. These emotions may also include pleasure or pain. They include anger, fear, pity, and the like with their opposites." Emotion is a heterogeneous area that covers a wide range of psychological phenomena. Some emotions are extremely specific, in that they have an effect on a particular person, circumstance, or object. Some are very general like sadness or joy. Some sensations such as sudden shameful feelings or rage may seem brief and hard to notice. Some sensations can last for hours or months and may even last years. An emotion, such as a facial expression may have pronounced accompanying physical effects, or it could be invisible to observers. Like a person "wallows" it, emotions can require conscious perception and thought. However, they can also pass almost unnoticed by the subject. An emotion might be significant in that it is important for one's physical survival or mental well-being, or it could be minor or unimportant. An emotion may be appropriate or not in a particular social context. Sometimes, it is socially required to feel guilt or sorrow after committing a criminal offense.

There are many feelings. And there is a lot of variance within different "emotion families." Fear and panic are separate feelings. There are many emotions that can be characterized as anger, such as rage, hate and resentment, disgust or loathing, scorn, and indignation. These emotions, in terms of their structure and context, are strangely different from members of the self critical family. This includes shame, humiliation. guilt. remorse. The wide variety and abundance in emotions suggests that there may not be one class of psychological phenomena. It could be that the emotion group includes a range of mental states or processes that are all connected.

Researchers and laypeople often segregate emotions into positive and negative. Scientists refer to these features as "affective values." However, this is not a good way to describe the complex emotions. Even though love and hatred are commonly viewed as opposing polarities, it is important that we recognize that they often coexist as complements. Aside from the fact that love can sometimes be painful or damaging, hate is often positive.

This classification is futile because anger, another "negative emotion", illustrates the futility. Rage can be either a negative emotion or violent towards another person. But it can also be an edifying emotion for those who are angry and can have beneficial effects in a situation or relationship if done correctly. Feminist movements made significant progress when women realized they had the right to feel angry and that there were a lot to get angry about. Aristotle observed that although feelings can be accompanied either by pleasure or pain, most often both, they are too nuanced to be defined solely on that basis.

The study of emotions has been a core part of ethics since the beginning. Aristotle believed emotions were essential to morality and that they were part of the medieval Scholastics' concern with virtues, vices, sin. Aristotle believed that virtuous behavior was possible by displaying the right amount in the right situations. St. Thomas Aquinas drew a distinction between the "higher" emotion and the "lower" emotion. The former was represented by faith, devotion, and anger, while the latter was displayed by envy and rage. While emotional extremes, malformations, and psychopathology have been associated with moral thoughts about emotions, like in psychopathology. Madness and madness have never been the main reason for emotional interest. Emotions are fundamental to a healthy person's life, which Aristotle and other medieval moralists recognized well. It is also why they can be so dangerous.

A person can live well and feel happy when they have healthy emotions. Emotions such as affection, empathy, and compassion are essential for interpersonal relationships. Emotions influence moral behavior (as well to immoral), and they are an important component of innovation and scientific curiosity. Many people feel triggered or provoked by beauty found in the arts and in nature. Without feeling, there can be no artistic sensibility.

Psychologists have long recognized that the fundamental processes of perception (and memory) shape emotions and physical sensations. These affect how people view the world and make decisions. While there are some feelings that can be out of control and affect one's social interactions and well-being, the majority of feelings are functional. The fact that so many people have "emotional issues" throughout their lives makes this a persistent societal concern.

The Structure of Emotions

Emotions have been extensively studied in many scientific fields including neuroscience, genetics and psychology. Different viewpoints on emotions have developed, which are related to the intensity or diversity of these emotions. Yet, it is important not to view these diverse viewpoints as a competition but as complementaries, as each provides insight into the different "structures" or feelings.

Emotions are not amorphous feelings. Their structured nature is questioned if they aren't structured. Emotions, however, can be structured in many other ways. This includes the way they are organized by the decisions they make and how they are assessed, their underlying neurology and the wider social contexts in that they occur. And finally, by the action that expresses them. Depending on the emotion, its condition, and its form, different emotions can show different structures at different levels and in different ways.

Experiential Emotional Structures

American psychologist Michael James presented the theory of emotion. James added one caveat. James states that perception is the initiating source for emotion. James does not accept awareness as part and parcel of feeling but clearly recognizes it's meaning. James understood that emotions had to be "about" something. It is not a physiological disturbance-based experience. James also referred to intentionality. This is the characteristic of certain mental processing that are fundamentally about or directed towards an object. James's analysis was revised by many of theorists that included perception and with it intentionality. Some philosophers argue that emotions can be defined as one type of experience.

As such, the definitions of emotional awareness have been substantially expanded to include more than just physical perceptions of what happens in one's body. It also includes perceptual impressions regarding what is happening in the world. However, when studying emotion, the viewpoint is both an emotional perspective that is "colored" by different emotions as well the subject's personal perspective. The metaphor of "color", which is a traditional metaphor for emotion, does not do it justice.

Emotion is not something distinct from or somehow overlays an experienced; the emotion itself is part and parcel of the experience.

Intentionality is the first element of emotional structure. It also includes what the emotion is about, such as a person or event. The subject's belief system and evaluative judgments regarding the event, the situation, or the subject in question are the main components of intentionality.

Many theorists have attempted to define belief in emotion. Others have tried to identify the "cognitive" emotions theories. While others focus more on assessment, these theories can be somewhat similar. However, their primary focus is on conviction, rather than evaluative. Although it is easy to understand the meaning behind "feeling" emotions, the essence of them is more complicated than what Jamesian views.

Emotions refer to awareness of the universe, values, thoughts and desires. Also, feelings must encompass not only physical emotions, but also cognitively rich perceptions and interactions that allow for learning, caring, and interaction. An emotion's experience dimension is not limited to its physical stimuli. However, it also includes the specific insight gained by that emotion and the experience of an object in relation to its environment. A person's experience of anger towards another person, for instance, is often based on their view of the situation. The experience of being in love involves the person's view of themselves as unique, loving, and worthy of treatment.

Rage and love memories can also bring out different feelings, memories, and the desire to behave in certain ways.

Aristotle stated that emotional experience is often about pleasure and suffering, but it rarely refers to isolated emotions. More often than not, multiple emotions are pleasurable/painful. It can also be pleasant/painful to have thoughts and memories. You can feel either pleasurable (e.g. It can also be an expression of pride or remorse. One can therefore understand that one may feel a certain way: happy to be in love again, or angry at oneself for making others jealous. The reality is that emotions can be complicated. It is perfectly normal to have mixed emotions.

Darwin believed some emotion expressions are due "the constitution of nervous system" and are essential for survival and adaptation. But, Darwin believed others have a different function: to convey emotion to others. In fact, they communicate emotions to other members of the group or species. It would be difficult to grasp the uniformity of expressions that signify emotion if this were not the case. One displays friendliness (and possibly an absence of intent to inflict injury) by smiling, the other is frowning. Emotional gestures, which are first forms of contact between a mother-infant at birth and the very beginning of infanthood when communication can only be done verbally, serve as the basis of emotional contact. Darwin observed, "We easily perceive sympathy in others through the expressions of our fellow human beings; our sufferings become lessened." We laugh together and share our good humor, increasing our joy and strengthening our friendship. The social component to emotion is most obvious in public displays that affect the actions of others. This element is not limited to contact. It also requires the social constitution (or social construction) of feelings with and through other people. The social structures and meanings of emotion are the relationships between triggers, content of speech, modes of speech, sense, and context. Social factors also affect fundamental emotions that are often believed to have neurological cores.

In an apparent sense social context determines the causes of emotions. Different situations in different countries can lead to different emotions. For example, fear caused by a voodoo sham may be felt in one culture, but it can also cause mild amusement and interest in another. In one society, jealous husbands may see their wives in the company and become jealous in another. All feelings are dependent on cognition. Many of the moral principles and evaluative thoughts that affect them are taught, but not all. It is up to each person and community to determine the appropriateness of the principles of right or wrong, appropriate or inappropriate, and their proper application.

Emotions, in terms of their speech patterns, are subjected social shaping. That is, most expressions, even those that are more hardwired, are subjected local "display rules," which determine which emotions and expressions are acceptable under which circumstances. Although it is totally unacceptable in Japan to have a rage attack in public, it is quite normal in urban areas in the United States. Socially, an emotion's cultural meaning is often defined. Rage, considered dangerous and even demonized in Tahiti is also a symbol in the Mediterranean of virility, which is a sign of righteousness. This does not mean their cultural perceptions are limited to emotional effects.

These interpretations can be used to create the emotions, or at least a part of them. Socially-constructed emotions can be more basic than those that are cognitively rich, such as moral outrage and romantic passion. However, history, along with nature, social differences, and individual differences, will determine which emotions are present and when.

Emotions as well as Rationality

The fact that emotions include actions and feelings raises the question of whether or not emotions can be considered logical. Plato, David Hume and others considered this a controversial topic. They thought emotion and reason were opposites. While actions and thoughts can be rationally or irrationally governed by society, the latter is able to impose its own rational rules. At most, these criteria allow you to evaluate overt emotion and thoughts.

People act and think irrationally when they get angry. It is rare that people feel stressed because they are strategically effective in channeling anger into positive action. But frustration can cause very rational actions and thoughts. You can find specific information in your frustration thoughts. This includes recollecting past wrongs and a pattern of aggressive conduct. Culture dictates what expressions and thoughts are acceptable. It is perfectly acceptable and reasonable to be jealous in some societies and circumstances. In other societies, or in other situations, envy is not acceptable and often irresponsible.

In two additional senses, emotions can also be rationally or irrationally. They can be more or lesser precise in their interpretation of the situation. And second, they can be more/less justified in their assessment of the situation. This is an example of the second scenario: Person A may be upset at Person b for saying something offensive. However, Person b actually did not say it and there is no reason why he would. One example of the second scenario is that Person A is mad at PersonB for saying something offensive. However,

PersonB's criticism of PersonA was fair and accurate, so PersonA should not be offended. The first scenario is absurd because it is based a false belief. In the second, it's irrational because it involves an unjust and unfair judgment.

Emotions, while logical in one way, can also be rational in another. They are functional in the same way. The idea that emotions evolved with humans is commonplace in psychology. It has been argued that they are the result if natural selection. However, it does mean that not all emotions have been selected individually for their roles in the past. Indignation could have been a useful trigger for violence in prehistoric times. But, in urban settings it may be dangerous or sometimes dysfunctional. Also, emotions can result from other characteristics. However, the general rule is that emotions play a large role in both the personal and interpersonal lives of people. Modern neuroscience has also confirmed the same conclusion.

Emotions can be rational, if used in a rational way to achieve basic human purposes. It is possible to be angry and help yourself overcome difficulties. In love could be a major step towards improving one's ability to maintain and form romantic relationships. While it's understandable to get upset at one's employer, it's also possible to become irrational when it frustrates one's career goals. While jealousy may be justified by a Buddhist monk, envy can also be irrational because it is against his Buddhist understanding.

Emotions are both the substance and ends of a life that is good. Jean-Paul Sartre was a French existentialist philosopher who argued that emotions were strategies. People use them for exploiting others and, most importantly, to control their thoughts and behavior in ways that are compatible with their image of themselves. The culture of emotions is a part of our lives, as well as the actions and attitudes we take over time. Therefore, it is up to us to control how they are perceived. It is possible to create or discourage emotions by prepping oneself to respond differently to certain situations. Aristotle believes that this kind teaching is part and parcel of the process of developing moral character. He concluded that having the right feelings and the right conditions is key to morality and human well-being (Solomon 2019.

Scientific Research on the Impact of Emotions On Perception

Psychological Science, an association journal, has published research that shows how emotions can impact what we see. Two studies found that people saw smiling faces more when they were accompanied by a positive image.

Erika Siegel of University of California San Francisco and her coauthors believe that people perceive actively.

"We don't simply react to the information we see in the world, we make it our reality.

Researchers explain that our affective reactions are key to how we perceive the world. "We don't get to know the world by only using our external senses. Our perceptions are influenced by how we feel.

Siegel, along with colleagues, found in their previous research that the first perceptions they had of neutral faces were altered by manipulating people's emotional states. This changed how they perceived faces as trustworthy, reliable, likeable, trustable. They wanted to test whether altering the emotional states beyond consciousness could have an effect on how neutral face perceptions are changed.

The researchers presented stimuli without participants' knowledge using a technique called continuous Flash Suppression. 43 participants were presented with flickering images. The images alternated between a blurred image and a neutral one. A low-contrast image with a neutral, smiling or scowling image was shown to their nondominant. This stimulus will normally suppress the image and make it difficult for participants to see. At the end of each trial, five faces were displayed and the participants selected the one they liked best.

The face shown to the dominant eyes of the participants was always neutral. Participants tended to choose the faces with the biggest smiles, even if the image outside of their consciousness was showing a person who smiled rather than neutral or scowling. In a second experiment the researchers used objective measures of perception and asked respondents to guess what orientation the suppressed face was. In subsequent experiments, only those who correctly predicted orientation at higher than chance levels were included in the study. Researchers found that participants misinterpret the appearance of positive faces as neutral.

Studies frequently show that decisions and actions are affected more by negative stimuli than those made with positive ones.

Therefore, this study's strong impact on positive faces is intriguing. Siegel and her colleagues point out that their findings may have wide-ranging, real world implications. This could be from everyday social interactions to more serious cases, such as when judges or jury members are required to determine if a defendant feels remorseful.

These studies prove that what we see does not reflect the whole universe. Instead, it is a conceptual rendering of the world as infused with our emotional experiences.

Chapter 4: Social Psychology

It is not an easy task to give a comprehensive description of nearly any field. This complexity is increased by two variables when it comes to social psychology. These are the large field's scope and its rapid rate for change.

Social psychologists are interested in many different areas. Despite that, most social psychology researchers focus on understanding how and why people act, think, or feel in social situations. This includes the symbolic and actual presence of others. So social psychology is the branch of science that studies how social contexts influence individual thoughts, actions, and emotions. Another way to say this is that social psychology examines how other people's social environments or thoughts affect our feelings, emotions and behavior.

Social psychology is a discipline committed to science. It attempts to understand how social action and thinking work. It is therefore natural to consider it science in orientation. However, non-scientific disciplines make statements about nature and people without being subjected to the thorough tests and examinations of the scientific community. It is possible to draw conclusions in areas like astrology or aromatherapy using intuition, confidence, as well as unobservable powers, which is contrary to what social psychology requires.

What Social Psychology Suggests About Self Identity

William Shakespeare wrote, "All the planet's a theatre, and all men and women are merely players."

This is a social psychological term that means we are all challenged with the challenge of presenting ourselves in a variety of ways to different audiences. Facebook and other social networking sites are a prime example of this preference. You have two choices: you can disclose most of who you are, as well as photographic documentation of your activities on Facebook. Or you can restrict who has access to that information to some extent (e.g. Setting privacy controls so that photos and wall posts are only visible to official "friends", allows us to limit who can access them. Is it possible to monitor what others discover about us and the conclusions that they draw? Do we really know enough about ourselves to allow others to be more accurate in predicting our behavior and knowing more about us?

There are many factors that lead to the conclusion that individuals truly know themselves better. We all have access, in some way, to our internal thoughts, feelings, or other mental states. It is obvious, intuitively, that we all have access to our own thoughts, feelings, and other mental states. But is it true, or are there other reasons? Research has proven that having access to our intentions is one of the reasons we make mistakes about ourselves. However, observers don't have it. Take the example below. Shirley, my neighbor's, is always late for anything. She always arrives more than half an hours late. I cannot count on Shirley being on time when I pick her up. You may already be acquainted with someone like her. Would she describe themselves as this? Probability not. However, you may wonder how she could know this for her self. It might be because she understands her intentions and knows how hard she puts in to achieving the target. This knowledge may lead her to believe that her efforts are mostly on time. At least in this aspect, could I say that she knows me better than I?

Although she does not know herself, I can probably predict the outcome of her actions in this case better than she.

These are just a few examples of people who believe they know better than others. But, paradoxically, others may also think they know better about themselves than they do the others. It has been difficult to research this subject because individuals have their own perceptions. These behavioral self reports aren't an objective way of assessing accuracy.

Shirley might continue with the Shirley example. She would likely state that although she may be late, she does her best to be punctual and she may even be able to recall a few instances when this was true. But, such behavioral self reports may still cause us to be suspicious. The new research has provided a solution that at least addresses the problem.

Researchers developed a more objective way to collect data by having respondents wear a digital voice recorder with microphone that recorded ambient sounds during their waking hours. Four days of recording was done at an average rate of 12.5 minutes. From these data, a measure of how a person acts on an everyday basis was made. The sounds were then coded by research assistants using a range coding systems that identified interactions with others, as well as negative emotional displays and other activities.

Before the actual conduct of each participant

was evaluated, they were asked about their daily activities and to rate themselves on their level. Three trusted informants, such as parents, friends, and romantic partners of each participant (e.g. These researchers also recruited three informants who were intimately acquainted with each participant (e.g.

It was not uncommon for the rating of a participant to be more directly related to their actual behaviors, but it was more often that the ratings of others were more closely related than the participant's own behavior. It is possible for people to "know us" better than we do or predict our behavior better.

Self-Knowledge in Social Psychology

Now we are moving towards some of the techniques that help us learn self-knowledge. An easy way to do this is to simply examine yourself. Another option is to look at yourself from the perspective of someone else. For self-judgment we look at the ramifications, then we examine what social psychological evidence has to say about how we can learn more about ourselves.

A key technique people believe is helpful for learning about themselves is introspection. It is the ability to take a step back and think about what it is that makes us unique. According to self-help books, millions of people read them every year. They believe that looking inward is how you can truly know yourself. Many believe that self-understanding can be achieved by looking deeper into our motives.

The several introspection-oriented books of this kind that are on the market tell us that self-inspection is the path to self-knowledge. Is this the best way of getting a complete view of oneself?

First, significant social psychological research shows that we aren't always able to understand or gain conscious access as to why our behavior is the way it is. Despite this, sometimes we can come up after the fact with rational explanations as to why we behaved the same way. Because we may not always know why our feelings are the way they are, we can create false explanations which could lead to incorrect conclusions. Experiments on introspection have shown this to be possible. Participants were asked to reflect on their emotions and to identify their reasons.

As you would expect, regrettable choices and inferences can result from relying on only other factors. Asking questions about why we act can cause us to lose our self-knowledge. Our own self-introspection may lead us to believe that we can predict our future feelings. We might be able to see how we would feel if we moved to another place, were fired from our jobs, or lived with someone for several years. We cannot predict how we will feel in these hypothetical situations if they aren't happening yet.

It is a mystery why we can't predict how we will feel in the future. If we focus only on what happened and try to predict how it will affect us in the future, we can easily lose sight of all the other variables that will likely impact our happiness. People believe that their future will be much worse than the one they have. Also, if we are able to focus on only one happy event in the future, then we will interpret our happiness as significantly higher than what is actually happening one year later. The problem with projecting our reactions to the future to these optimistic events is that we don't recognize the everyday obstacles that we are likely to face in the future. This will affect how we actually feel.

Let's examine another direction that our introspection can take us. You might be able to decide whether it's easier to spend money on gifts for others or on yourself. If you are like most people else, you think buying cool stuff for yourself will make it happier than buying gifts for others. But new research shows the exact opposite. Spending money on other people makes us happier than spending money on ourselves. In a nationally representative study of Americans, respondents were asked to rate happiness and to compare how much they spend on their own expenses and gifts with gifts for others. Although people tend to spend more on their own than they do on others, the main question is what predicts satisfaction.

According to the researchers, happiness is not directly related to personal expenditure. However, spending more on others can lead to greater happiness. This observation held regardless of people's income. It was evident that there was an added bonus to giving to others, whether you are wealthy or poor. One could argue that this was an analysis that looked at similarities. However, it's not possible to be sure that the outcome will match our expectations. Spending on others has causally contributed to respondents' satisfaction.

Researchers conducted a basic, yet informative experiment. They conducted a morning survey of psychology students and gave them either $5 or $20 to use by 5:00 p.m. that day. Half of the participants were told they could spend the money themselves on a personal gift or bill. The other half were told they could give it to charity.

Which group was happier, at the end,? It didn't matter how much money was given, the participants who gave their money to others reported significantly higher satisfaction. This experiment proves that how we choose to invest our money matters more than how much. Participants were asked to choose which scenario would bring them greater satisfaction. People who tried to predict how their feelings would be indicated that they would rather receive $20 than $5. These self-predictions didn't prove accurate. This shows that we do not know how events will impact our lives and that simply reading into it will not help us understand how events affect our feelings, actions and thoughts.

Self-identity from the Perspectives of Others

As we know, it is possible for other people to be more accurate in predicting what our actions will be than we are. You can think of yourself as an observer by looking at your own history. As observers have different levels of concentration and are less likely than others to be affected and understand our motivations, they may be better able predict how we will behave in future. We instead focus our attention outside as actors and attribute more circumstances to our behavior. Observers focus on the actor directly and assign more dispositional explanations to the same actions.

If we consider ourselves an observer of ourselves, we are more likely to define ourselves in dispositional, or characteristic terms. These were the results of a survey asking people to identify themselves five years ago and today. The present self was seen as different from all contexts, and was less often described in terms of general arrangements. This was true irrespective of age or length of pasts. Both college-age and middle-aged participants viewed themselves (as analysts tend) in terms if they were consistent in describing their past self relative to the present self.

How do we perceive ourselves as observers influence how we think about ourselves, and how can this help us to self-insight. Researchers used several types of acting techniques as a way to investigate how how viewing ourselves from the viewpoint of the observer influences how we see ourselves. The participants were divided in two groups and given "acting instructions." The goal of the "method-acting" class was to make the participants "feel like they were the other person."

The "standard acting" group asked participants to put on a performance that would make them appear to be this person.

In this case, everyone saw their past self through one of the following perspectives:

The one group was instructed by the other to depict their past self with the viewpoint of someone experiencing it. The central measure for interest was again the number or consistency of traits or dispositions that were used to describe their 14 years old self. The answer was obvious. The method-actors were more actors-like and perceived themselves in terms only of a few consistent traits. While those who played themselves with a more "observer actor" perspective saw themselves in terms more consistent traits. As we try to see ourselves through the eyes of others, we tend to have more consistent behavioral tendencies. If we try to see ourselves through the eyes of others, and accept that they might be more accurate than ours, then self-insight can be achieved. Is introspection always misleading? It depends on our concerns. If the action involved is based in a deliberate decision-making procedure and not on implied emotional considerations, it could well lead to correct self judgments to consider those motives.

Introspection can't lead to self-inferences. We don't consider the variables that influence how we feel. While looking inward might be helpful in certain situations, it could lead us astray. Many people are able to provide reasons for why they do certain things. But, they might be using self-theory as a basis for explaining their actions. These theories may be useful, but we can still not see the real reasons behind our actions.

Most people do not know how emotional events affect them. Studies have shown us that, instead of dwelling on the good things that have happened, we can think about how those same positive results could have been avoided. It is possible to draw some conclusions about one's thoughts, motives, habits, and feelings.

Social Identity vs Self Identity

According to the Social Identity Theory, depending on where we are on the personal-versus-social identity spectrum, we will view ourselves differently at any given moment in time. Personality is the most important part of this spectrum. We think of ourselves at the social spectrum as individuals who represent particular social classes. It is impossible to simultaneously experience all aspects our self-concept. Therefore, how we perceive ourselves at any given time will determine how we think about ourselves. In terms of how you view yourself and how you react to others, the momentary salience, or the portion of our identity at the center, can have significant impacts on how you see yourself.

Our personal identities are often popularized and we see ourselves as special individuals. This causes self-descriptions to emphasize the differences that other people have from us. As an example, if you think of yourself at the personal identity level, you might find yourself describing yourself as pleasant. This is to show that you are more like other people who have this trait. Personal identity self-description may be seen as an intragroup comparison that involves similarities with others in the group. In this way, our self-descriptions of the personal self may have an impact on the content.

You might be asked to explain what makes you different from others. Now think about what your definition of yourself would look like. If you were asked to describe yourself by comparing yourself with your parents you might say you are particularly liberal. If you are comparing yourself with other college students, it is possible to view yourself as quite conservative. The argument is that what we make to define ourselves, including for our personal identity, can be affected by how we perceive the world. In this case, it could result in us seeing ourselves as either liberals or conservatives.

As members of a group that is at the social identity end, we should emphasize the things we have in common with our fellow members. We can describe ourselves in terms the characteristics that separate our group from any similar group. Intergroup Comparisons are, in essence a description of oneself at the level if social identification. This includes distinctions among groups. If it is important for you to identify as a member in a fraternity, sorority, or other community, then you might assign yourself characteristics you share with the members of your group. A group that exhibits agility and self motivation can stand out from others fraternities or sororities in your area.

Gender is an important social identity. If your gender is dominant and you are female, the qualities that you identify with others (e.g., warmth and caring) may be interpreted by you as self-descriptive and used to differentiate women from men. In the same way, you may self-stereotype as a male. These are characteristics that are used to describe men and make them different from women. You should remember that your self-description can be different from when you think you are a member a group with other people. This is because you may not see yourself as an individual. Most people belong to many groups. These can be defined as gender, age, profession, sexual orientation or ethnicity. However, not all of them will be the same and our importance may vary. If a social identity is important, people are more likely be to act in a way that reflects that part of themselves. It is possible to have many different situations that influence how we see ourselves. As such, the behaviors that are influenced by these self-definitions may vary. There are many ways to describe ourselves at any one time. This can result in multiple "selves." You're not wrong. Even though self-definition is prone to change, most people maintain a cohesive view of themselves. We recognize, however, that there are many contexts in which we might describe and act differently. This can be due to the fact that domains in which our views are contradictory may seem unimportant or not significant.

How Self-Identity Impacts Behavior

So how do identity and personality as well as our attitudes as a consequence of them influence our behavior, according to socio psychology?

Most likely, you've encountered a difference in your behavior or attitudes on several occasions. Because of the influence of social context, the relationship between attitude & behavior will be affected. What would be your response if someone shows you a brand new tattoo they are proud of and you ask for your opinion. You might say you don't like the tattoo if it was your opinion. Chances are that you wouldn't want to hurt the feelings or friends. Therefore, even if it's negative, you might say you like. These situations are where we know that our decision to not act on what is true to us is clear. This illustrates that behaviors can be differentiated from actions depending on their social consequences. The consistency of your attitude and how you react to the tattoos of your mate can tell if you will get it.

Recent research has focused both on the factors that influence consistency, and the impact of attitudes on actions. Because of the crucial role that the social context plays in determining how behavior and attitudes will be linked, recent research has also looked at the factors that affect when consistency can reasonably be expected. Many factors influence the degree of correlation between actions and attitudes. In other words, the environment can impact how much attitudes will determine behavior. It is important to note the characteristics of the attitudes as well, like how confident and positive you feel about your own attitudes. When compared to attitudes that we doubt, attitudes that we maintain with greater confidence are stronger linked to actions.

People can be induced to believe their attitudes will remain consistent over time. They feel more confident in these attitudes and more likely act on them. It is well-known that people older than their peers are more confident with their behaviours than those younger. Recent research suggests that older people have greater confidence in their actions than young people. They are also more likely to remain consistent with their attitude-behavior. Are you worried about what people might think of your attitude to a problem if it isn't true? If you do, you will be able understand the problems faced in a Stanford University study. They had negative views about heavy alcohol intake. They assumed that the attitude to heavy alcohol consumption of other students was more positive than theirs (a case of pluralistic ignorant, when we mistakenly believe people have different attitudes from us). When the students were randomly selected to find out more about the alcohol attitudes and beliefs of Stanford students, they found that the students felt more comfortable talking about alcohol to other Stanford students than they did. Also, they varied in how comfortable they felt about expressing their opinions about alcohol to another student. Students had greater ease talking about campus drinking. In fact, they chose this subject for discussion more often if they thought that other students were more supportive of alcohol

101

than they were. However when they discovered other students' attitudes towards alcohol were more negative than theirs, they were less inclined to do so. This tendency for students to be supportive of their campus group but not to change their attitudes was especially intense for those who identified strongly with them.

Spontaneous Behavior and Identity Based Attitudes

When people have the time and space to examine all potential actions they may make, their ability to predict future behavior is strong. Sometimes, however people must respond quickly to certain situations and their responses can be more spontaneous. Imagine a car cutting in front and not giving you a signal. These situations tend to affect behavior in a more direct and apparent automatic manner. Motives play a less significant role. According to Fazio's attitude–to–behavior theory, the method operates as follows.

An attitude can be created by any event. Our ability to determine what is acceptable and how we view different social norms is enabled simultaneously. Our definition of an event is formed from our mentality and our previously stored knowledge. This understanding impacts our behavior. Let's give you an example. Imagine someone crashing into your lane of traffic while you're driving. This incident will alter your attitude toward people who engage in dangerous and uncourteous behavior. It also affects your perception about how people should behave on expressways.

The behavior will be seen as non-normative. It can also impact your reaction and understanding. You might wonder "Who is that person thinking?" In other cases, your response may be more situational. "What a nerve!" "Gee," or "Gee, he/she must have been in a great hurry!" Whatever the event interpretation, it will affect the individual's actions. There are many studies to support this view. These are two mechanisms that influence our actions. However, they work under very different circumstances.

We are often too busy to make this sort of analysis and many people's reactions seem faster than they can be explained. These situations are where our behaviors can have a direct impact on our perceptions of different events. Habitual practice and the formation of a pattern can make it easy for a person to respond in a predictable manner when faced with the same situation.

Induced Compliance Behavior

Many reasons may lead us to engage in attitude discrepant actions. Some are more persuasive then others. Which will shift our behavior more: When there are "good" reasons or when there's no reason to be attitudinal? Cognitive dissonance says that dissonance increases when there are very few explanations why we do not engage in attitudinal actions. Because we are unable to rationalize our actions to others, dissonance could be quite severe. Participants were initially asked to perform repetitive tasks on the first test, such as turning pegs on an overcrowded board.

Half of the participants were promised $20 and $1 respectively if they revealed the fib to the waiting participant. After performing the "favor", the participants were asked what their feelings were about the boring task.

Participants who were paid $20 considered the task less challenging than those who were only paid $1. The participants who were paid $20 could have had a legitimate reason for lying, but it was not the case if they were given $1 to repeat the same lie. If you are not given a reason for your actions or if your situation is more valid in the $1 (than the$20), condition, then you have to reduce your dissonance. So what can individuals do to decrease their greater dissonance under the $1 condition? They alter their cognition, which causes the issue.

The lie you stated in this example cannot be changed. In other words, you can't deny your behavior. However, by making the boring job more exciting, and reporting that your mood was more optimistic in the $1 scenario than in the $20, you can prove it wasn't a liar. Cognitive dissonance theory says that people can modify their attitudes more easily if they are given only enough to induce them to adopt attitude-discrepant behavior. Social psychologists refer this unexpected prediction to the less-leads - to-more impact-less explanations of a behavior or incentives that can lead to a change in attitude. Numerous studies have confirmed it.

Indeed, the more people are given money or other benefits to support their attitude-discrepant behavior, the more they can justify their actions and could even lead to them being disowned. Coercion would be a way to reduce dissonance. Also, small incentives lead to more positive attitudes when people feel responsible for choosing the right course of action and any negative outcomes. We may not experience dissonance if we do not feel that we are responsible for our choices. A dissonance example would be when an authority directs us to do an activity that is contrary to our personal views.

Social Psychology is a way to impact the behavior of others.

Group Influence

Scenario 1 You're studying for an exam when a cell phone rings. What do you do now?

Scenario 2, You're driving and you hear an ambulance siren approaching your vehicle from behind. What do YOU do?

Scenario 3 You are standing at the supermarket checkout and the one right next to you opens. Who is going to be first in the new check-out line?

In all these situations, it is possible for the people involved to act in certain ways. You can only guess with some degree of certainty what the other person will do, though similar etiquette exists.

Students with loud phones would quickly turn off their phone and apologize to the students sitting next to them. If you hear an ambulance coming, pull over to your left and possibly stop the vehicle before it arrives. The checkout line can be a little more tricky. The long checkout line may seem like the easiest. However, it is not. You could beat them by someone else from the back. Most individuals can anticipate higher compliance in contexts with more obvious norms, as opposed to situations such as this, where the norms are less specific on what behavior is the "right one." It's not difficult to predict what will happen next.

These and many other conditions lead to strong results. The way conformity presses us to do the right thing in a situation is an example of how this works. In other words conformity is the pressure we feel to act in ways that are compatible with laws. These laws are called social norms. They often have strong effects on our behavior. The confusion in the checkout queue is caused by the fact the standards for that situation are not as clear as those in the other. It isn't clear whether people can go in front or behind the current line.

Social norms are clear and comprehensive. In many cases, government works by written laws and constitutions. Chess has very specific rules. There are signs that outline what actions to take (e.g. stop! ; Avoid Swimming and Parking; Do Not Leave the Grass. This is true in many public places like airports, parks, and highways. You can also consider the rising trend of restaurants displaying different tips on their bills, such as 15 percent or 17 percent or 20 percent. These numbers create social norms for tipping. Research has shown that tipping rates are higher when they exist than when they don't. The norms could be implicit or unspoken in other contexts. They may also have evolved in an informal way. We all know such unstated guidelines like "Don't shout during a concert" and "Try not to make noise when going to interviews." It doesn't really matter whether formal or informal social expectations are implicit or explicit. The majority of people will follow them nearly all the time. Practically everyone, regardless what their political views are, stands when their nation's national anthems are played at sporting events. The same goes for restaurants. Very few people tip the waitress. This social standard of excellence is so strong that most people tip the waitress at least 15%, regardless the quality of their service.

At first glance, conformity can seem incontemptible. It is a strong desire to conform and follow the guidelines of society or a group on how we should act under different circumstances. It can, however, restrict individual liberty. However, the basis for this much conformity is very clear: without it we will be facing rapid social turmoil. Imagine what would happen to people who don't adhere to the "Forma line and wait you turn" norm in places like movie theaters, arenas or supermarket checkout counters. You should also consider the potential dangers to pedestrians, drivers, and cyclists if traffic laws didn't exist. In certain cases, however, conformity plays an important role.

If you have ever been to a country in which traffic laws are not strictly enforced or are treated as merely suggestions, you can understand why we say that people act out of social expectations. This can make it dangerous. Another reason people conform is to look good to others, or to give off a better impression. Many people believe that conformity facades give them the appearance they accept their company's values and priorities.

For example they might make statements they don't really believe or suppress personal beliefs. They also keep secrets about their private thoughts. They might find it difficult, but it is important for their careers.

Encourage compliance

Robert Cialdini a social scientist was convinced that researching compliance practitioners would help you find out more about compliance. Compliance practitioners are people who have the ability to get others (financially or otherwise) saying yes. These are the people. This group includes advertisers, government contractors, fundraisers as well as salespeople, special negotiators, scammers, legislators, and politicians. Cialdini took lessons from these people by concealing his true identity for a while and then found work in diverse environments to attain compliance.

In other words, he worked in sales, fundraising, advertising and other compliance-focused fields. These first-hand observations led him to conclude, however, that even though enforcement strategies may take different forms, all of them can be based on six principles:

Friendship/liking. We are more likely to give in to requests from our friends and family than from strangers and people we don't like.

Commitment/consistency: When we have committed ourselves to a position or action, we are more likely to comply with demands for actions that are compatible with this position or action than with requests that are not.

Scarcity: We are generally more concerned about the outcomes or items that are less available or becoming scarcer and will try to get them. It is therefore more likely that we will respond to scarcity requests than those who are not.

Reciprocity. If someone has offered us a favour or concession in return, we will usually be more willing to oblige. Also, in other words, we feel compelled, in some way, to pay them back for the service they have provided.

Social validation. We are more willing to comply with an order if it is compatible to what we believe others are doing (or thinking). We want justice, and one way to do that is by thinking and acting like other people.

Authority: In general we are more ready to comply when someone holds legitimate authority.

Cialdini explains that these universal concepts provide the basis of many ways practitioners can achieve compliance with each other.

Can You Still Be Influenced By Someone Even When They Aren't There?

It's not surprising that other people can manipulate us while they're present. They have many strategies at their disposal to get our thoughts, words, and actions to suit their purposes. Even though they may not be present, and aren't trying to influence our actions or feelings in any way, growing research has shown that others can have an effect on us. While the evidence is not new, the principle is. Floyd Allport, who wrote perhaps the first social psychologist textbook, described influence as "the effects of others' real, imagined, or implied presence on people's thoughts.

In the end, we are responsible for creating these outcomes. Other entities, however, do not produce them. Although we don't know it, our mental impressions of others -- what they like or dislike, our relationships and how we feel about them--can have powerful influences on us. Researchers found that when they were subliminally shown the faces of their intimidating department chair, graduate students had a tendency to be less positive about their own research ideas. Graduate students didn't consciously see the chair's face, but it was visible for a very brief time. His pessimistic facial expression influenced their opinions of their work. How does our behavior and perceptions impact the psychological existence of others, as shown by our mental images about them? Two systems seem to be involved. Both of these systems can also include our goals. To the extent that other people are present within our minds (even if we are not aware), this can lead to relational schemas, mental representations and relationships with those individuals.

In turn, these relational plans may allow for specific objectives to be activated. In other words, when we think about a friend we might activate the goal of being supportive. If we think back to our mother and father we might trigger the goal that we make them proud. These priorities will impact our actions and thoughts as well as our assessment of others. If the goal of being physically attractive triggers our desire to help others, then we will be more useful. If we have the ability to be attractive physically, and are offered the delicious dessert, we may turn down the offer.

Second, we may be drawn to certain goals by other people because of our psychological connection. This, in turn will impact our ability to complete different tasks successfully and our commitment to reaching these goals. If we think of our dad, and know he wants us to be successful in college, then our commitment can be increased. This is especially true for those who are very close to him. To put it another manner, it is possible stimulate the essence our relationships with others, the goals that we pursue in those relationships, or the goals these individuals want us achieve. These ideas, information systems, will have a significant effect on our actions.

This effect has been observed in many studies. One such study involved asking individuals to think about a close friend or a coworker at an airport. After being asked to identify the person they were thinking about, they were required to write down their initials. They also had to answer a series question about that person (e.g. describe their appearance, how long they've known them, etc.). Next, participants were asked if they would be willing to help the researcher. This was done by answering a long series of questions. Participants who thought of a friend would be more likely help the researcher. Because thinking about a friend will bring up the need to assist which is something we would normally do for friends. This is exactly the case: More people were able help if they thought about a buddy than a coworker. Not that they were asked to support their friend but rather a stranger or researcher. But, their actions were influenced by their thoughts about their friend.

As you can see, there are significant connections between identity/personality and human behavior as a result of social psychology. Although all schools of thought offer different points of view about the development and evolution personality and identity, it makes perfect sense that human interactions will influence the development of "self" (Baron & Branscombe, 2014).

Chapter 5: Cognitive Behavioral Therapy

Now that you have an idea of how your identity develops and changes over time, which personality types we have and how you can identify them, and how social psychology considers our identity and personality to influence our behavior, you can begin to solve problems. As we know, identity and personality evolution can face many challenges. Some of these could be trauma-related. However, it is common to simply want to address various aspects of one's behavior and live the life you envision.

There are many treatments that we can use to change our behavior and create the lifestyle we desire. Cognitive Behavioral Therapy is one example.

What is Cognitive Behavioral Therapy and how does it work?

Cognitive Behavioral Therapist (CBT), is an evidence-based treatment that identifies and addresses psychological disorders. CBT practitioners can be clients, but not all CBT professionals are doctors.

CBT can be described as a structured, active type of therapy. Clients are guided through the process of counseling in order to determine their goals. CBT is founded on four core principles.

1. How people perceive the environment and how it affects their thoughts, feelings, reactions, and behaviours. Clients should interpret their concerns in terms their feelings, desires, behavior, and physical responses. This will help them understand their problems and support their solutions.

2. CBT clients will learn to recognize their emotions and be supported with CBT interventions to change their opinions.

3. Clients can alter how they think to change their emotions and physical responses.

4. As thoughts, feelings, reactions and behaviors are interrelated thoughts,

emotions, behavior, and behavior can also be affected as clients change their thinking.

CBT was developed first in the 1970s to treat depression. Rogerian was, Gestalt, and Psychodynamic remained the most common therapeutic orientations. CBT was an entirely new approach, which combined a focussed framework and active discussion to help people understand their thoughts.

Many hours of research over the past 50+ years have examined both the fundamental hypothesis and the utility of CBT to children and adults. CBT can help with a range of issues. For example, it can teach you how to deal with stressful situations and how to manage anxiety. CBT does not require any medical diagnosis.

It may also assist with:

Understanding how to manage extreme feelings like frustration, fear, or sadness

The solution to your sorrow

Manage mental illness symptoms and avoid relapses

Coping with health problems

Resolving disputes

Strengthening communication skills

Training for assertiveness

CBT may prove to be beneficial for a range of conditions. This includes:

Anxiety disorders

Addictions

Chronic pain

Bipolar disorders

eating disorders

Depression

obsessive-compulsive disorder (OCD)

post-traumatic stress disorder, (PTSD)

phobias

sexual disorders

schizophrenia

Tinnitus

sleep disorders

A CBT Session

CBT sessions always start with a check in. Practitioners and clients review their progress and discuss areas for improvement.

Second, create an agenda for the session. Also specify the topic.

The third step in the process is to go over the agenda with the client and address their concerns.

CBT: The Building Blocks

CBT's building blocks are feelings, thoughts. Physical reactions. Behavior.

It can be overwhelming to experience anger and sadness. It is often difficult to pinpoint the root cause of our anger, so we tend to blame others. Imagine Rose, a CBT Client. Rose is twenty five-years old. She has been living at home since childhood and just finished college. She is currently trying to find a job. Rose received another letter of rejection yesterday. Rose spent the night alone in her bed, feeling extremely sad, browsing the internet, and crying. Rose tells her CBT doctor the next morning that she is feeling depressed after she lost the job. Rose is normal to be upset. Of course, Rose would feel differently if her job was awarded. Rose's reaction is likely to be a mixture of emotions and physical reactions. She's carrying around a lot of stuff in her large backpack. CBT will be required to assist Rose in unpacking the bag.

She will open the bag and take out her emotions, reactions, and actions. This is called the "four-factor model." The four factor model is a framework that both you and the CBT practitioner can use in order to understand the variables involved in your problem. People who have context for explaining their answers tend to feel less overwhelmed, and they believe it is easier to make progress. Unpacking makes the backpack lighter. Rose will start to consider what she will take on the journey, how she wants it to change, and the things she does not need. Rose will observe her responses, attitudes and thoughts and place them on the floor in tidy piles.

Rose can use the four factor model to determine her reaction once she has unloaded her backpack.

Situation: Another rejection letter was received.

Rose's Thoughts

Rose's feelings are hopeless and depressed.

Rose's physical reactions include stomach pain and exhaustion.

Rose's Behavior was: Rose stayed in bed crying and surfing the Internet. She also skipped gym class the following day because she was too tired. She didn't apply the following day for the job that was advertised in The Paper.

Rose will feel less overwhelmed once the backpack of thoughts is empty.

The four-factor model is able to distinguish between behavior, emotions, and feelings. The objective truth or what actually happened is called the situation. A forthcoming test for instance is a situation. However, a "hard" forthcoming examination is a scenario. This interpretation would indicate that the exam will be difficult. Let's use another example to illustrate the point: A client tells CBT that he was confronted outside school by a young boy who said "You're ugly". If this person adds "That kid's mean and trying show off," then that is their interpretation of what happened. The reality of the situation does not change, but the interpretation will impact how the person looks at it and how they feel.

The Difference Between Thoughts, Feelings

The four-factor model is designed to help you distinguish emotions and thoughts. While it may sound simple, our daily language seems to make it difficult. So, when we say, "I feel like the man doesn't want me," it really means, "I don't think that he likes me."

CBT is hard to master because of our tendency to confuse emotions and thoughts. Feelings are usually described by one word. Thoughts are often expressed as sentences or phrases. CBT refers specifically to the automatic thoughts we have in particular situations. Your automatic thoughts occur very quickly and are just below your conscious awareness. Thoughts depend on how or what we perceive a situation as to us. You might be approached by a man on the street asking for directions. If you are adamant that he is trying mug you, you may begin to try to get away.

But if your first instinct is to assume he's just a lost tourist, think about all the ways you can help and be friendly.

Automatic thoughts can be words or images that are sent through our brains. Many of our automatic thoughts focus on things that are very common, like I wonder if there will be rain today. Or Do I have my shopping lists? When you leave the home. These thoughts usually don't provoke strong emotions and aren't something we pay attention to in CBT. CBT tends to be more interested in thoughts that can lead us to feel negative. For example, I may think nothing of myself and have a negative thought about others. However, my mother might think that I am inconsiderate. My thoughts about the future might say, Everyone will laugh at us. These thoughts are typically below your consciousness level. However you might be able to ask yourself what I thought. These thoughts are usually easy to recognize.

Automatic thoughts are effortless and spontaneous. There are many of them. And they can come and go quickly, so we don't notice. It is possible to begin to observe our thoughts and to begin to change them. If we have positive thoughts, our feelings and behaviors change.

The difference between Physical Reactions, Feelings, and Behavior

Changes in the body can be described as physical reactions (e.g. tension, sweating or tingling). Intensive emotions follow physical responses. It is sometimes difficult to identify the emotion from the body's response. An example of this is anxiety. Your heart rate could increase and you might feel a lot more nervous. Individuals might experience similar emotions, but may react differently to them. Individuals' physical reactions can vary in strength. A CBT client may be able to provide valuable insight by asking about their physical reactions and how strong they are. Sometimes people are conscious of their reactions and feel them. This can be a great place to begin understanding your feelings.

People have different feelings about how they feel about their body. Is it possible to feel uncomfortable about your physical reactions, such as blushing?

What we do is called behavior. It is important to recognize behavior as a separate factor. This allows you to begin to examine how the other two factors affect your behavior, and the consequences of your behavior. If we don't alter our behaviours, we will continue to experience the physical effects of our thoughts, emotions and reactions.

Are Thoughts able to Maintain Problems

Our feelings and understandings of the situation relate to our emotions as well as our physical reactions and actions. Rose thought she was so disappointed that she wouldn't get a job when she got the rejection letters. If these are her thoughts, it's easy to see why she feels depressed and helpless. If she had thought, "I'll try again" and that something would happen, she may have felt neutral, or even slightly positive. Different thoughts contribute to distinct emotions, behavior, and physical responses. It all starts with a particular scenario. How we perceive the situation immediately influences our feelings. These emotions then contribute to our actions, physical reactions and emotions. We will try to keep emotions and physical response in the same place for the time, as they are so closely tied.

Let's take a look at one example of how thoughts influence emotions, physical responses, as well as behavior. Shady is a very sweet black dog. Despite my best efforts, Shady barks furiously each time I come home. I don't pay much attention, and he'll soon stop barking. He's so adorable. I am happy to see him even though he is barking. Alicia, a great friend of my, comes over for a stroll. Alicia is going ring a horn, Shady is going to bark and Alicia is going think, He's gonna jump all over me, get me dirty. Dogs are unpredictable. Alicia feels nervous and stressed. She is not pleased to meet Shady. As a direct result, she avoids the dog.

How behavior can cause problems

To understand your behavior and the effects it has on your emotions and feelings, as well as your physical responses, you need to find out how your behavior contributes to your problems. Consider the consequences of your behavior. Let's explore the ways that thoughts can be strengthened by the consequences. Second, let us examine how the consequences for a behavior could impact the situation, in order to reinforce original ideas.

Let's say Alfred is a seventeen-year old boy who takes a math test. Here is an example using the four-factor model to describe Alfred's reaction. Alfred thinks the exam is too hard and he'll probably fail. He becomes anxious and has a headache. His behavior is to go home and play video game.

What do his thoughts and what does the situation say about Alfred's behavior in this instance? Alfred did his homework, but the exam was not passed. He claims that the test was "too difficult" for him because he failed. And he thought that it was going to be a failure anyway. The test failing proves that the test was difficult. Therefore, his original thoughts become validated by the consequences. Alfred never gets to test his prediction of failing anyway. He might not have passed if Alfred had studied. However, it is possible that he would have passed even if he did. He will see his defeat to be confirmation that he will "fail anyway."

Now let's see how Alfred's actions influence the situation. Alfred failed the examination. The content might not be understood. The fact that math concepts depend on each other makes it more likely for Alfred to fail the next test or perform poorly. As a result, his actions shift the realities of his lives to make his negative thinking more likely. This is what CBT practitioners refer to as a maintenance cycle for symptoms.

Do Core Beliefs Infuse Thoughts

It is a set of fundamental beliefs that are solidly held and can cut through all kinds of contexts to affect your automatic thoughts.

CBT books may use the term schema. The core beliefs and schemas are virtually identical. There are generally three types or core beliefs.

Clear Life Rules. Clear life rules are guidelines on how life should go or how the world works. They can have very little affect on your emotions. Examples may be:

Respect strangers.

You will be able to succeed in your life if you have the right education.

Your life jacket should always be worn on a ship.

Intermediary assumptions, convictions. These laws can be expressed in the form of statements if...then...I. These laws play an essential role in deciding how we feel and what we do. Examples may be:

I won't be able to succeed unless I'm perfect.

People will listen to my shouts if they hear them.

If people can see me real, then they'll be condemned.

Core beliefs. These beliefs can be held about oneself or others. They are general and absolute statements, which can be expressed in a few phrases and that are very powerful. Core beliefs can either be adaptive or destructive. It can be difficult for people to recognize them and make changes, as they are not like automatic thoughts. Examples may be:

Self-focused core beliefs: I am clever, I am lovable, I am greedy, I am incompetent, I am unlovable.

Core beliefs about people: Others are kind, other will take care, others will be there for me, some are mean, and they will exploit me.

A core belief about the universe: The world's justice and security are its foundations, while the world's peril and injustice are its main features.

Although an individual's core beliefs are affected by his nature, they can be altered by later life experiences.

CBT can help you to understand your strengths

Finding your own strengths can be difficult. Recognizing that you are not a magician is one way to find your strengths. Let's imagine someone saying that their son was "lucky" because, after his internship he was asked back to work full-time. Consider what is required for a young male to be called back for a job full-time after an internship. Will a fairy goddess ever tell a young man, "Here are the jobs for you"?" The woman's husband had to show up to work on schedule, work hard, have a pleasant disposition, and be punctual. These are just a few of the many strengths that her son has. Even though he was lucky, luck is rarely enough.

Here are some questions you can use to identify and think about your strengths.

Are there areas of your life where things are going well? I don't mean just being able and willing to overcome obstacles. But it also means being able or able, in general, to maintain a consistent routine. You might be able to get up at the right time each day, get your kids ready, and then have dinner ready for your family. It takes time, effort, organization, and perseverance to accomplish this feat. It is important for you to look at your strengths as you go about daily tasks. It might be helpful to reflect on the strategies you use to persist in daily tasks.

Have you been able complete developmental duties? Did you manage to maintain a steady income, have good friendships, pass your school exams, or even get a job? These achievements show you are able keep promises, have new knowledge and have great relationships with other people.

Do you live with an animal or a person? Caring relationships are about loyalty and putting others' needs aside.

Are you being consistent with your principles and objectives? It can seem daunting to act according to your values and principles.

Are you an expert in a particular subject? People are endowed with many successes and talents. A person doesn't have a great deal of success to be knowledgeable in one area. Perhaps you are the person who bakes birthday cakes most often or provides computer support to your friends. People can learn coping techniques that allow them to thrive in these particular areas and apply them to other areas of life.

Identifying negative spirals of behavior

CBT involves understanding how we arrive to the behaviors we wish to change, and what our triggers are. Different situations can trigger a person's negative behaviors. It is essential to recognize which circumstances can cause you to behave negatively in order to find solutions.

Some people are aware of their causes. However, others have difficulty identifying their triggers.

A person may tell you that they are always depressed and/or drink too much. The trigger for their behavior can't be identified. Identifying the reasons helps us see trends and identify what to address in therapy. First, it is important to identify any troublesome emotions or behaviors and track them. Next, look for instances when they are more extreme or more common. Tracking the events in which your anger is strongest, for example, can help you determine if you feel "always upset". Tracking your emotions can help you discover when anger is most intense. For example, if your teenage son breaks his curfew or fails to do his homework. You can feel the anger spreading to other areas of your lives. The trick is to get rid the overriding labels and replace them with specific acknowledgments of situations in which the problem has been at its worst.

The more specific you can make the situation clearer, the better. Emotionally involved in the situation can help you feel more open and honest. Imagine a friend with whom your irritation is mild. Now, recall a time when this person upset you. Try to remember the details. When you think about a situation, chances are you will become more annoyed and have more immediate thoughts and emotions. You will experience the same effect if your thoughts turn to other situations. The situation may be complex and can sometimes seem like a long story. It is possible to replay the entire story and then ask yourself, "What was the most frustrating?" It's best to only identify situations that last between 10 and 30 minutes. Longer situations will lead to a variety of emotions and feelings. This will make it hard to concentrate on the essential emotions.

Identify Your Feelings

To be able to recognize your emotions and manage them in a healthy way is part of emotional control. When you ask "What was the feeling?" you're telling yourself to pause, think and take stock. This helps to stop the negative spiral. It allows you to identify your emotions and keep track of them. Your emotions can also influence a CBT session. There are different ways to approach CBT depending on your predominant emotions. First, you might not know where to start if "bad" is what you are experiencing. But if "anxious" is what you feel, then you can begin to explore the fear and anxiety behind it.

Identify your Physical Reactions

Your emotions are also guided and influenced by your physical responses. There are many ways to misinterpret your physical symptoms. This could lead to emotional distress or dysfunctional behaviors. One example is that someone may believe he is having an attack of the heart if his heartbeat is irregular or dangerous. He becomes anxious and avoids situations where his heart pound. His pounding heart is not harmful and can be explained by excessive coffee consumption. It is difficult to understand the meaning of your physical reactions until you are able recognize them. Some people are acutely aware of their bodily reactions. Others are unaware. To understand your physical reactions, it is important to ask yourself: "How did the body respond?" Or, "What did I feel inside my body?"

It can be helpful to start by recognizing your bodily reactions, then move on to identifying emotion if you have trouble identifying them. You might also find that certain emotions have specific physical responses. It is possible to find out, for example, that you are hot if you feel frustrated or anxious. Or, that your body reacts differently when you feel happy. It is easier to recognize your emotions if your physical symptoms are linked to your feelings. This helps you become more self-reflective by helping you identify your physical reactions.

Identifying your Behavior

Next, you need to understand what your behavior means. You need to ask yourself this question: "What did it mean?" If you have a tendency to avoid, act impulsively, and/or behave in a manner that is likely aggravate the situation, then you should be asking yourself what you did. For some, it's a first step towards recognizing the problem behavior and taking responsibility. Maybe you have problems managing your anger, or you want to lessen your anger. Your actions can be described as "letting off steam", when you describe how annoyed you were at a friend who didn't repay a small loan. When you remember what you did, however, and how hard you kicked the door, you may be tempted to blame your friend. He didn't pay the debt. This could make you even more angry. It is possible to recognize that this behavior wasn't caused by the actions of your friend and can now understand that you are trying reduce it by saying "letting out steam".

To understand your behavior better, you want to provide a clear and concise summary of all your actions. You may then be able to determine whether the reactions were appropriate and what the implications are. Initial statements can be vague, such as "I just gave it up" or even "I freaked." It's important to question what you really did (Josefowitz. 2020).

CBT: How to Impact Behavior

The theory behind CBT states that your thinking patterns have an impact on your feelings. This can in turn affect your actions.

CBT illustrates the negative effects of negative thinking on emotions and behavior. Reframing your thoughts positively can help you to feel more positive and encourage more supportive behaviours. Your practitioner will teach you how to make lasting changes in your daily life. CBT can come in many forms, depending upon the problem and your goals. You may need help:

Identify and fix any problems you are having in your day to-to-day life

Recognize and change unproductive patterns in your thinking.

The ability to recognize and reshape toxic thinking in a manner that changes how you feel

Learning and putting in place new habits

After a consultation with your CBT practitioner, you will be able to determine which strategies are most effective to achieve your goals. We will talk about nine CBT techniques to help you change your behavior.

1. Cognitive Reframing or Structure

This includes looking at negative patterns of thinking. Perhaps you tend over-generalize, believe that the worst is coming, or assign too little information too much significance. This way of thinking will affect what you do, and can even result in self-fulfillment. CBT practitioners will sometimes ask about how you think so that they can help you identify any negative patterns. If you become aware of these negative feelings, you can learn how they can be reframed in a way that is more constructive. A good example is "I blew the project because I'm completely ineffective" which can be transformed into "That report wasn't me best job, but it was a valuable work and I contributed many ways."

2. Guided Discovery

CBT professionals can help you to understand your viewpoint by using guided discovery. They will then ask questions intended to challenge you and expand your thoughts. Sometimes they may ask you for evidence to support your assumptions. The process will help you see things from different perspectives, even ones you might not have considered. This will help you choose a path that is more rewarding.

3. Exposure Therapy

Exposure therapy can help you overcome anxiety and fears. Exposure therapy can be used to help you deal with anxiety and fear. This can be achieved in small steps. Your coping skills will improve as you become less insecure.

4. Journaling and Thought Records

Writing is a tried-and-true way to express yourself. In CBT sessions, your CBT provider might ask you to record negative thoughts and to suggest positive alternatives. It is also a good idea to write down the new concepts and habits that have been established since your last session. It's a good way to keep track of how far you've come, and put it on paper.

5. Activity Scheduling und Behavior Activation

It can be helpful to make a calendar entry for any activity that you would rather put off or postpone because of anxiety or fear. You might be more likely not to put off the activity until it is over. It is important to plan events so that you can establish healthy habits and have enough opportunity to put in practice what your learned.

6. Behavioral Experiments

Behavioral experiments are commonly used to treat anxiety disorders which can lead to panic attacks. Before you take on a mission that normally makes you nervous, you will be asked what your predictions are. You can then assess if your prediction came true later. As you get older, you will start to notice that the disaster you expected is unlikely to come true. Start with less anxiety tasks, and then build from there.

7. Relaxation and Stress Reduction

CBT can teach you some progressive relaxation techniques, such as:

Deep breathing exercises

Relaxation

Imaging

You'll gain practical skills to ease tension and improve control. This can be helpful in coping with phobias, social anxiety and other stressors.

8. Role-playing

Role play can help you manage stressful situations with a variety of behavior. You can reduce anxiety by acting out scenarios in the future.

Improve problem solving skills

In some situations, building trust and familiarity may be necessary.

Social skills

Training for assertiveness

Strengthening communication skills

9. Successive approximation

This can include taking on tasks that look daunting and breaking them down into smaller pieces that are more manageable. Each step builds on previous ones, so you gradually gain trust.

What is Catastrophic Thinking exactly?

Particularly for those suffering from anxiety and depression, catastrophic thinking may be a significant behavioral problem.

Catastrophizing means that someone believes the worst is possible. Sometimes it is a way of thinking that your problems are worse or you are exaggerating the severity. An individual may worry about whether they'll fail an examination. If they fail an examination, they may conclude that they are a bad student, and they will not pass, graduate, or find a job. It is possible that they believe this to mean that they will never have enough money. It is possible to fail tests and still be successful. This does not mean that you cannot find a job. For someone with catastrophic thinking, this would be very difficult to grasp.

Over-exaggeration can lead to catastrophizing, which is easy to overlook. However, it's rarely intentional. Sometimes people who do it do not realize why. It can make them feel like they have no control over the things that worry them. In this case, their health might also be affected. There are helpful psychotherapies.

It isn't known exactly what causes catastrophism. It could be a coping method that a person learns from other people or relatives. This could be from an experience, or the brain's chemistry.

Researchers found evidence that individuals who are extremely impulsive and also suffer from chronic pain have higher activity in their hypothalamus/pituitary reactions, which are the brain areas that record pain-related emotions.

Cognitive behavioral treatment is effective in helping people change their behavior. It is important to recognize that no single approach will work for every person. Therefore, it is best to look into other methods of behavior alteration.

Chapter 6: Human Psychology and All or Nothing Thought

By distorting reality, we block any other way of seeing an event. A party can either be a great success or a complete failure if it is guided only by our emotions. A single criticism can be considered an all-out attack upon our character. We can be either completely superior, or completely sub-par. It's not surprising that anger and depression are linked to all or nothing thinking. We feel sad because the world seems out of control. And we are angry because we don't think we can do enough. It's a life with no grays.

When our focus is on everything or nothing, we tend to think of the extreme. Perfect or imperfect. Good or poor. Femme fatale. Saint or demoniac.

An all-or nothing mentality is often reflected in a distorted mind's vocabulary. Words like "always," the "no way," the "perfect," the "evil," the "horrible," the "disastrous" or "should-be" are second nature to someone who thinks this way. In this way, the all or none thinker judge themselves and others. The 99 percent remaining are worthless and meaningless if something isn't 100 percent. Can this be a cause of disappointment for both oneself and the people with whom we are associated?

Peter is an attractive, successful account manager who hasn't been able sustain a meaningful relationship even though he desperately wants one. Problem is, he only can deal with a relationship if it meets all of the terms and conditions. This is not likely to be possible. Brenda, an attractive young woman, was a friend of Peter's at the gym. Peter regularly visits the gym six days a semaine, in pursuit of the perfect body. Brenda asked him out to a movie. Peter considered that Brenda might just be the one for his life. They went on their second date to a dinner. He was eager to show his knowledge of wines. His spirits soared when she told him she was impressed. Brenda ordered the lamb tagine, a Moroccan-style meat stew. It is hard to believe that someone like her could eat dead animals! Peter was a strict vegetarian. He tried the lentil and the couscous. However, he was disappointed that he could not enjoy it. Brenda seemed like a good choice, a perfect match. He felt she was not understanding the issues. He could help her understand them and show her the wrong way. Peter left Brenda a message a few days later. He waited to see if she would call. There was no call back. He didn't even think about the possibility that she might have missed the message or had been out of town for a few business days. Peter was certain that it was over. Another downfall in a relationship. He didn't even think of double-checking Brenda and accepting her different eating habits. Peter saw it as all or nothing. Accepting anything other than what is required would be unacceptable.

Cognitive-therapy has been extremely successful in identifying distorted thinking without any gray areas. It can be useful to share your thoughts with someone who is stuck in a binary world of black and blue. Tell the person to use "and" in place of "or" when describing them. An example: A person can be a meat eater and good. This mental shift allows you to think in a way that is less rigid and more flexible. It opens up other options.

Thinking all or none effectively divides your mind into two categories: the present and the future. This mentality is caused by great insecurity. It's subconscious, and all or nothing thinkers are often unaware of the reasons. Most likely, the distorted thinking pattern starts in childhood. When we are told that our mistakes are unacceptable or that we are stupid for not having an answer immediately, it is very common. This way of thinking can lead to a negative view of ourselves and our surroundings, which can then be extended into adulthood. Our behavior is still controlled by undeveloped, infancy thinking.

When faced with such thoughts, the countermeasure is not to be negative or perfect. Although there are always exceptions, these occasions are rare. Most people's lives are all shades of gray. If a writer doesn't make the bestsellers list, it is still a author, and most likely an excellent writer. The person has failed to achieve one goal. This is far from the definition failure. Or, a successful dietter has eaten an entire sundae of ice cream. The black and blond thinker will not remember all the healthy meals or the lost pounds and will instead fixate on one thing.

We don't need to think in terms of all or none. All or nothing thinking will only make us more anxious and put us in a flight or fight mode. One error or imperfection can trigger panic. Then we run and leave the entire situation. Because the danger is real to the distorted mind, this reaction tends to be immediate. It is not possible to "let's hope and see" for the distorted thinker.

You should not be drawn into the world of such a distorted thinker. The good news is that you can still make mistakes. This is essential to understand because distorted thinkers may cause others to question their own judgments or take blame for them. Ask yourself what the situation is. You might be called a fool by someone who thinks erratically. Ask yourself: What logic does this lead to? How did all your wonderful qualities suddenly disappear from your life? Uncertainty cannot be tolerated by the distorted thinker. Everything must be obvious immediately. If you cannot please this person, it's not your fault.

Encourage the black or white-thinking person you know to explore other options. The fallacy of using words like "always", "never", and "always," is highlighted. If someone complains that he/she has "always had bad luck," challenge them to see the positive aspects in their life. The simple fact of being alive is a major plus. Anybody who has enough food and shelter to live comfortably is blessed.

Ask your friend questions they may not have considered.

Can an intelligent and well-informed person make a wrong decision?

Can you still love someone while being angry at them?

Can someone love me without getting mad at me?

Is it possible for a job to be both fulfilling and fun?

As we'll see later, all or none thinkers commonly use labels as a way to define themselves and other people. A person can be described as either a republican or democrat, religious or atheist or blue collar worker, executive or vegan. These labels provide a convenient shortcut for those who are rigid thinkers to define themselves. It's a "we," versus "them" mindset that eliminates any possibility of compromise. It's also very time-saving, as it doesn't need to take into account any other person's view. A lack of clarity can lead to lazy thinking.

Here are some ways you can convince an all-or none thinker to explore other options.

1. A person should not associate self-worth with achievement. As achievement can vary daily, the link between self-worth and achievement can lead to anxiety. This is because even high achievements one day can be anxiety-provoking as the person recognizes that things can change very quickly. Instead of focusing only on achievements, build character traits like honesty and reliability, kindness as well as a strong work ethic. These qualities are a true indicator of a person's value.

2. Hypercritical all-or-nothing people are invariably critical. There is a lot of insecurity hidden beneath the mask. It is part of the territory. It is important to remember the positive characteristics when dealing with someone. All people have them. Hypercritical

people don't see the positive or dismiss them as insignificant.

3. Restrictive thinkers tend to limit your options. You should consider other options. It doesn't matter if you disagree on a movie. There are many things you can do together.

4. If someone uses rigid labels such republican or democrat to describe you, ask them whether they agree with the actions of their group. There is a good chance they won't. This can make it easier to accept others and be more flexible.

Chapter 7: Human Psychology and Overgeneralization

Overgeneralization is the most dangerous type of distorted thinking. Overgeneralization simply means that the characteristics of a restricted number of individuals are extended to the entire group. Sometimes that can amount simply to bigotry. Most of the time it's more complicated.

Overgeneralization is thinking (or reasoning) that involves all or nothing thinking. It includes everything, everyone, and no one. It can be even well-intentioned, but also harmful.

Tony is a concerned dad to two teenage daughters. Tony is a good father. It's clear that he wants the best for his teenage girls and to keep them safe. Tony feels dread every time he sees a news story about a teenager being hurt. Tony's mantra is, "It wouldn't happen, my girls." Tony claims to be a good and protective father, but he won't let his daughters go out on dates. He must always be able and willing to help them. Other children are not allowed to stay at the house unless their parent is present. Tony does admit to feeling guilty but still goes through their phone and social media accounts. He says that he does it to "protect them". He will do almost anything to protect them from pain, disappointment, and unhappiness.

Tony understands that there will be teens who get in trouble. He also believes that all teenagers can become disaster-bound. Instead of teaching his daughters from their mistakes they prevent them from repeating them. Instead of encouraging them to confront their fears or doubts, he insists on ensuring that their lives are free from fear and doubt. Tony is raising two fearful young girls who will be ready to face their reality. He has learned from a few teens who had been in bad situations and has now applied his experience to all teenagers. Tony refuses not to see the large majority of teenagers that blossom and learn social skills from their parents. Tony understands that being a parent can be difficult. He is making the easy choice by making sure his girls are not faced with any difficulties, make no difficult decisions and have plenty of lessons to learn. Their daily messages are that they shouldn't trust their own judgments or themselves.

Overgeneralization leads us to think of people and other entities as if they were all or nothing. "Men have more reliability than women." "Jews can always be trusted." "All corporations do not work well."

This is a common way of thinking that can lead to racism and discrimination. This is the logical consequence of judging an individual based upon the behavior of random numbers of a specific group. Let's focus on "Men make better workers." The person who tends to overgeneralize will be happy to point out his "proof". This Joe in the office has not missed a day of work in years. Lisa does miss work when she's needed.

Let's examine this "proof". Joe hasn't missed one day of work. But, Joe is a plotter, works slowly, and rarely contributes original ideas. Lisa is single and misses work occasionally because of her son. She compensates by working late when it is necessary, getting more done, and being willing to help others. However, none of these things fit the mold of our over-generalizer. So, he rejects the notion that both women and men can work hard. He knows better.

Most negative overgeneralizations have a purpose. It's fear-based thinking. When we are able to classify and label any individual without knowing much about him, then we know who the bad guys really are. It tells you who it's safe to make friends with and who to avoid. The hard work has been done. It takes away all the uncertainty that distorted thinking cannot handle.

Three possible methods of overgeneralization:

First, you take a representative of a group and make a decision regarding a whole group. Tony, the great father. He is well aware that not all teens are good. He rationalizes from this, but he doesn't consider the fact that every teenager will get in trouble. Imagine a man losing a promotion due to a woman having slept with the boss. He is obviously bitter, and he has come to the conclusion that all women gain success through sexual favors. A single negative incident has enabled this man to form an opinion over an entire group.

However, it is easy to be too general about ourselves. Let's not forget the little blonde who we met at our party at beginning of the book. She would have attracted a few men to her, and that attention led her to conclude that all men find she irresistible.

It is possible to also overgeneralize by using large, representative groups that don't actually represent the group. Many poor immigrants begin their lives in low paying jobs. That is true for centuries. But, the over-generalizer thinks there is a lot of immigrant laborers, and concludes that all immigrants should be working in low-paying service jobs.

If you mention an immigrant who's an attorney or doctor, you will be told that it's an exception to prove the rule. Over-generalizers do not like being challenged about their deep-rooted certainty.

We all enjoy a certain amount certainty. The overgeneralizer is a master of this. He or she has set up limiting beliefs about how things are and can't be done. When reality proves otherwise, they blame reality for not being reliable. Their all or nothing mentality must not be affected by anything.

Overgeneralization is a thought that can lead to negative thoughts about yourself, others, and even life. Therefore, it is crucial to pay attention and be aware of what your thoughts are and the ideas you work with. What data is your mind using to make its conclusions about the world?

Don't be afraid to ask someone for clarification and proof if they are being too general. Ask Tony, the dad, how many teenagers he does not think are in trouble.

Ask him how he expects the girls to prepare for actual and genuine adversity. It would make him think. A way to get along with someone like that is to ask him/her to express his thoughts in written form and find out how true they really are.

It takes perseverance. This may mean that the over-generalizer will agree to your point of view, but it won't be permanent. He or she will most likely return to the old ways of thinking when they have another chance to justify old beliefs. It takes time to change the reality of someone. It can be very beneficial for someone to broaden their perspective. People who believe that all women must sleep to be successful should not be able to point out women who are merit-based. Sometimes, reality is your most powerful ally.

The third method we use to overgeneralize our actions is by rationalizing it and saying, "But everybody does it." This probably happened when we were in grade school. Mom, with arms outstretched, stared at us.

"If everybody leaps off of a bridge, would they?"

Mom, score one. She was so right.

It's okay for a sevenyear-old child to try to get one past his mom. However, this is a common excuse for adults to be immature. This kind of distortion is so common, people even believe it. Our thought patterns have been altered by social norms.

People are openly revealing that they use this fallacy in logic for breaking rules they don't love. Proud, even. They boast or gleefully admit to distorting tax returns, falsifying insurer claims, and cheating in tests. It's what everyone does.

This thinking leads to the obvious problem that not everyone will do it. The rationalization is not more than an excuse to fail to do your best. It can also make you less of a person than you should or could be. "Everybody does this," drives you down to your lowest common denominator. Your perception of what everyone else around you is doing will limit your potential. However, you can be sure that you are dishonest and others will see. When you are distrusted by others, it's difficult to keep your self-respect intact and self-esteem.

It's not enough to just say that "Everybody does this", but you have to appreciate something more than the reward of cheating. This should be your character. It's knowing that you can take pride in who you are. It's watching people stare at you and thinking, "I wish we were more like him."

If someone comes at your with the lame overgeneralization that "Everybody does" then the right answer is, "No, not everybody."

Chapter 8: Human Psychology.
Catastrophic Thinking.

Ellen rarely opens her mail and doesn't answer calls from numbers that she doesn't recognize. It's not because she is too busy. She is quite the contrary. Ellen doesn't really have many friends, so Ellen is able to spend a lot of her time. It's not that she is overwhelmed by anxiety at the sight of unexpected mail or phone calls. Ellen thinks a phone call to work immediately means that the boss will be calling her with bad news. Mails can be any type of bad information, and make Ellen feel anxious at home. Even if they are a simple form from HBO. Ellen might get an email advising her of a deadly disease. Ellen might receive a phone call from a bill collector or the IRS. Even though Ellen does not owe anyone money, the IRS could also be calling. Ellen has a stack in her home drawer that is unopened with a few letters. Even if the worst happens, her doctor will inform her that she has a critical diagnosis. She won't be able to locate it in time. Ellen can only avoid reality.

Ellen suffers from catastrophic thinking. Her way of thinking is that disaster can strike any time. Freddy Kruger lurks in the background, waiting to strike at any moment.

Ellen's delusional thinking may have a reason. Her mentally unbalanced mother used to slap Ellen relentlessly as a child. She would shout, "If it hasn't done something wrong, it will in the future." This is a lesson. Ellen used to hide under the covers when her drunken father would storm into her bedroom at night. Ellen was always the "new child on the block", the bully and the picket because of her father's inability to keep a job.

Ellen discovered early in her life that bad events can happen at any hour. Thirty-years later, however she is still confined to the same horrors.

Bad things happen. People who are spouses to firefighters or police officers suffer from real anxiety all day. A tornado alert could cause enough anxiety and fear to require a family member to immediately seek shelter. These fears are not catastrophic and real.

Catastrophic Thinking is when we believe the worst, in spite of all logic and reasonable odds. It usually happens when there is no other cause. Anxiety can be caused by anything. When a presentation is due, someone with chronic anxiety knows that it will be disastrous. Catastrophic thinkers are often able to see everything before they go on their first date. A simple headache can quickly become a brain tumour by using catastrophic thinking. It is a tendency to dwell on the worst-case scenarios, which can make people fearful. It stops the person from being calm and working on possible solutions for anticipated problems. Instead, the catastrophic thinker becomes paralyzed by fear and makes it more likely that something will go wrong.

Breathe deeply, especially when panic attacks set in. Anxiety can cause shallow breathing. Our heart rate increases when our brain doesn't get enough oxygen. Simple breathing can calm your mind instantly. When you begin to notice your breath, your imagination of a catastrophic event will naturally diminish.

You are finding yourself calmer and it is time for you to evaluate the facts. It is a scary thought that you will be meeting your boss for a performance evaluation. You don't know what to expect. Besides, you have a strong feeling that he doesn't like or respect you. Take another inhale. Take another breath. What's the next step? To cope with anxiety, taking action, no matter what kind, is a great way to get your mind off it and glve you something to do. Make a list with all the projects completed since your last review. Keep track of the benefits you have brought to the department. You should also be ready for any negative comments your boss might make. Your attendance is not as good as it should have been. Write down and practice your explanation.

Your anxiety will be more realistic if your brain is busy making preparations and finding things to do. You won't feel completely out of control, although you will still be anxious.

To reduce the fear of meeting with your boss, imagine a positive experience. Put your head back and relax. Imagine your boss's office. Include as many details and details as possible. Look at the desk and the file cabinets. Take note of any photos that he keeps on a bureau. Next, take a picture showing the boss as he is usually dressed. Think of having a positive conversation. This visualization can greatly reduce anxiety and stress in stressful situations. It changes your perspective from the negative to the positive

An anxiety-induced situation can prove to be catastrophic. You have met this promising guy, he is actually employed and will let you in on the job. A call comes from him to inform that a group of his friends has just dropped in and would you be willing to meet them. Your immediate response is to tell him you'd rather go to the root canal or skydive with no parachutes. It's your first time meeting him. Do you want to make friends with him? No.

Your brain is buzzing with countless thoughts. When he gets to know and love you, you'll never be the same. His friends will see you as dull and boring. You're sure to say something outrageously stupid. You will most likely spill red wine onto his carpet.

It's time to take a deep breath. Now think about what the odds are that the man who called you is going to hate you. He must like something about you, so he'd pick up the telephone. Is that something you are not thinking about? Is it because you are boring that his friends think so? He didn't. Or he wouldn't be calling. For those who say something dumb, you have plenty of time to brainstorm some interesting conversation openings. That will at the very least give you something interesting to say. Asking questions can place the burden of conversation on them, rather than you. It's important to take some form of action to avoid your brain becoming overwhelmed by anxiety. If you don't want to drink red wine, white wine or Ginger Ale are better choices.

Focusing your attention on something you have to do and giving yourself an assignment keeps your mind busy enough to not get over-anxious.

Sarah, who is a legal assistant, recounts the interesting story of how two SEAL friend took her and several other girlfriends to a SEAL training site. They spent an enjoyable evening learning survival techniques. When she was asked what she was most afraid about, she stated that she was scared of becoming lost in dark woods. One SEAL told her to keep replaying her favorite songs in her mind if that happened. He said that while she would still be scared, her mind should be focused on the songs to avoid terror. Sarah was intrigued by the idea and requested a demonstration. She was left alone in the woods, at 3:00 in the morning, and in total darkness. (Although she could see that one of the SEALs was within 2 feet of her, she wasn't sure. Sarah felt terror and put her head against a tree. Sarah was utterly terrified. She'd never felt such darkness before. It was easy just to imagine being attacked wild and hungry animals. She then remembered what the hidden SEAL had said to her a few minutes earlier. Sarah, an avid Broadway musical fan, mentally scanned every musical lyrics she could remember. She acknowledged that he was correct. She admitted she had been scared but she had managed to keep her mind off her favorite songs and stayed calm.

If you are a person who is prone towards panicking and catastrophic thinking, then why not share the secrets of one of America's best-trained fighters? Although the mind may be a reliable computer and can handle multiple tasks at once, it is not able to focus on them all.

Chapter 9: Human Psychology.

Emotions have a positive effect. We need them. Unexpected gifts can make you feel very happy. People who care about you are ill can make you feel worried. Emotions can help you feel better. But emotions can cause people to get in trouble. Remember that emotions to our brains are still raw data. Emotions cannot be interpreted as right or incorrect. As such, they can be unreliable data that can be used to guide your actions.

When emotions are processed and considered valid, logic is used. This skill can be learned. A four-year-old child won't be logical. Even people in their twenties are capable of struggling. This is why older people tend to accept mistakes made by younger people more readily.

People make crucial decisions based on emotion and have no internal system to verify that the facts are correct. Fear of commitment may arise from your parents' bad relationships. If this is the case, you will avoid being close to people to prevent them from hurting. You feel alone, which can provide an insight into your situation. This allows you the opportunity to be critical and critically evaluate. Understanding the root cause of your lack of happiness can help you understand your parents. You can use both your emotions as well as your thinking to get important information. It is important to keep thinking, analyzing, and understanding in order to change negative emotions. If you don't, your thinking will become dependent on your emotions. This is very similar to a child. Emotions can be seen as reality to a child. I am mad so this person has to be mean. The child can't think about the logic of such an assertion. It's just a simple fact. If you are afraid of making a commitment, then your thinking is exactly the same as the child. You accept your fear as an accepted fact. As we grow and mature, our cognitive skills also increase. We are able to recognize our emotions and gain an understanding of them. This can eventually lead to a change in the way we think. This is maturing psychological state. It involves processing raw emotions into something manageable and controllable. In other words, it allows you to see the problem through new eyes and help you find a solution.

Emotional thinking refers to facts you already know. But, often your emotions influence those facts. It is clear that you know the history of your parents' bad relationships. You know this is not what you want for yourself. These two facts are what make you think inaccurately and emotionally. The moment you start to think critically or logically you are in control. To reach new conclusions, add more facts to previously known facts. Your mind becomes more open to new possibilities, as you add new facts. You begin to see how your emotional limitations have limited your ability and willingness to take positive actions.

Emotional reasoning isn't necessarily rooted in deep roots. It can affect our thinking. Emotions can be used to aid our thinking at any time. Robbie is currently a Stanford sophomore majoring on pharmacology. Robbie is a bright, intelligent man who can think clearly. His 3.9 grade-point average probably reflects his intelligence. Robbie experienced severe depression after breaking up his relationship with his girlfriend. He spent a lot of time watching television while he moped around. He completely forgot the important chemistry exam and was unprepared for class. He failed the test. Robbie didn't stay depressed after the breakup for too long. He started to study hard for his next Chem test. Robbie experienced anxiety and doubts for first time during college. The last test he took had been a failure, so how could he expect to do well on this one? Perhaps he didn't have what he needed to earn his degree. Is it really worth his time to study when he was likely to fail?

Robbie was blinded to the fact Robbie was a good student and had been emotionally vulnerable during the last exam. One failed exam was enough to make Robbie forget everything else. He was so focused on his failed test that he forgot about all the others he had taken and became completely oblivious of them. Robbie does not have the ability to observe his emotions calmly and add other relevant facts. This will make it more likely that he will fail the second test.

It is important to be cautious when dealing with an emotionally thinking person. People who are emotionally disturbed can be prone blame others. The commitment phobe will spend hours justifying their distorted thinking by blaming other people. Understand that you're not the problem if your relationship is with this person. The best thing to do is listen and be present.

Talk to your emotions to someone who is able to listen, but don't tell them to change. They will respond when they feel ready. You'll reap the rewards if you can support them during this time.

Robbie is a situational emotion thinker. This makes it easier to deal. Robbie's distorted thinking resulted from one event. This was an emotional overwhelm. Pointing out other relevant facts (such as all his other tests) will help him get back to logical thinking.

www.ingramcontent.com/pod-product-compliance
Lightning Source LLC
Chambersburg PA
CBHW060329030426
42336CB00011B/1262